Scott Foresman
Science

See learning in a whole new light

PEARSON
Scott Foresman

Editorial Offices: Glenview, Illinois • Parsippany, New Jersey • New York, New York
Sales Offices: Boston, Massachusetts • Duluth, Georgia • Glenview, Illinois •
Coppell, Texas • Sacramento, California • Mesa, Arizona

Series Authors

Dr. Timothy Cooney
Professor of Earth Science and Science Education
University of Northern Iowa (UNI)
Cedar Falls, Iowa

Dr. Jim Cummins
Professor
Department of Curriculum, Teaching, and Learning
The University of Toronto
Toronto, Canada

Dr. James Flood
Distinguished Professor of Literacy and Language
School of Teacher Education
San Diego State University.
San Diego, California

Barbara Kay Foots, M. Ed
Science Education Consultant
Houston, Texas

Dr. Shirley Gholston Key
Associate Professor of Science Education
Instruction and Curriculum Leadership Department
College of Education
University of Memphis
Memphis, Tennessee

Dr. M. Jenice Goldston
Associate Professor of Science Education
Department of Elementary Education Programs
University of Alabama
Tuscaloosa, Alabama

Dr. Diane Lapp
Distinguished Professor of Reading and Language Arts in Teacher Education
San Diego State University
San Diego, California

Sheryl A. Mercier
Classroom Teacher
Dunlap Elementary School
Dunlap, California

Dr. Karen L. Ostlund
UTeach
College of Natural Sciences
The University of Texas at Austin
Austin, Texas

Dr. Nancy Romance
Professor of Science Education & Principal Investigator
NSF/IERI Science IDEAS Project
Charles E. Schmidt College of Science
Florida Atlantic University
Boca Raton, Florida

Dr. William Tate
Chair and Professor of Education and Applied Statistics
Department of Education
Washington University
St Louis, Missouri

Dr. Kathryn C. Thornton
Professor
School of Engineering and Applied Science
University of Virginia
Charlottesville, Virginia

Dr. Leon Ukens
Professor of Science Education
Department of Physics, Astronomy, and Geosciences
Towson University
Towson, Maryland

Steve Weinberg
Consultant
Connecticut Center for Advanced Technology
East Hartford, Connecticut

ISBN: 0-328-10003-X (SVE); 0-328-15673-6 (A), 0-328-15679-5 (B);
0-328-15685-X (C); 0-328-15691-4 (D)

5 6 7 8 9 10 V063 12 11 10 09 08 07 06

Consulting Author

Dr. Michael P. Klentschy

Superintendent
El Centro Elementary School District
El Centro, California

Science Content Consultants

Dr. Frederick W. Taylor

Senior Research Scientist
Institute for Geophysics
Jackson School of Geosciences
The University of Texas at Austin
Austin, Texas

Dr. Ruth E. Buskirk

Senior Lecturer
School of Biological Sciences
The University of Texas at Austin
Austin, Texas

Dr. Cliff Frohlich

Senior Research Scientist
Institute for Geophysics
Jackson School of Geosciences
The University of Texas at Austin
Austin, Texas

Brad Armosky

McDonald Observatory
The University of Texas at Austin
Austin, Texas

 ## Content Consultants

Adena Williams Loston, Ph.D.

Chief Education Officer
Office of the Chief Education Officer

Clifford W. Houston, Ph.D.

Deputy Chief Education Officer for Education Programs
Office of the Chief Education Officer

Frank C. Owens

Senior Policy Advisor
Office of the Chief Education Officer

Deborah Brown Biggs

Manager, Education Flight Projects Office
Space Operations Mission Directorate
Education Lead

Erika G. Vick

NASA Liaison to Pearson Scott Foresman
Education Flight Projects Office

William E. Anderson

Partnership Manager for Education
Aeronautics Research Mission Directorate

Anita Krishnamurthi

Program Planning Specialist
Space Science Education and Outreach Program

Bonnie J. McClain

Chief of Education
Exploration Systems Mission Directorate

Diane Clayton Ph.D.

Program Scientist
Earth Science Education

Deborah Rivera

Strategic Alliances Manager
Office of Public Affairs
NASA Headquarters

Douglas D. Peterson

*Public Affairs Officer,
Astronaut Office*
Office of Public Affairs
NASA Johnson Space Center

Nicole Cloutier

*Public Affairs Officer,
Astronaut Office*
Office of Public Affairs
NASA Johnson Space Center

Reviewers

Dr. Maria Aida Alanis
Administrator
Austin ISD
Austin Texas

Melissa Barba
Teacher
Wesley Mathews Elementary
Miami, Florida

Dr. Marcelline Barron
Supervisor/K-12 Math
and Science
Fairfield Public Schools
Fairfield, Connecticut

Jane Bates
Teacher
Hickory Flat Elementary
Canton, Georgia

Denise Bizjack
Teacher
Dr. N. H. Jones Elementary
Ocala, Florida

Latanya D. Bragg
Teacher
Davis Magnet School
Jackson, Mississippi

Richard Burton
Teacher
George Buck Elementary
School 94
Indianapolis, Indiana

Dawn Cabrera
Teacher
E.W.F. Stirrup School
Miami, Florida

Barbara Calabro
Teacher
Compass Rose Foundation
Ft. Myers, Florida

Lucille Calvin
Teacher
Weddington Math &
Science School
Greenville, Mississippi

Patricia Carmichael
Teacher
Teasley Middle School
Canton, Georgia

Martha Cohn
Teacher
An Wang Middle School
Lowell, Massachusetts

Stu Danzinger
Supervisor
Community Consolidated
School District 59
Arlington Heights, Illinois

Esther Draper
Supervisor/Science Specialist
Belair Math Science
Magnet School
Pine Bluff, Arkansas

Sue Esser
Teacher
Loretto Elementary
Jacksonville, Florida

Dr. Richard Fairman
Teacher
Antioch University
Yellow Springs, Ohio

Joan Goldfarb
Teacher
Indialantic Elementary
Indialantic, Florida

Deborah Gomes
Teacher
A J Gomes Elementary
New Bedford, Massachusetts

Sandy Hobart
Teacher
Mims Elementary
Mims, Florida

Tom Hocker
Teacher/Science Coach
Boston Latin Academy
Dorchester, Massachusetts

Shelley Jaques
Science Supervisor
Moore Public Schools
Moore, Oklahoma

Marguerite W. Jones
Teacher
Spearman Elementary
Piedmont, South Carolina

Kelly Kenney
Teacher
Kansas City Missouri
School District
Kansas City, Missouri

Carol Kilbane
Teacher
Riverside Elementary School
Wichita, Kansas

Robert Kolenda
Teacher
Neshaminy School District
Langhorne, Pennsylvania

Karen Lynn Kruse
Teacher
St. Paul the Apostle
Yonkers, New York

Elizabeth Loures
Teacher
Point Fermin
Elementary School
San Pedro, California

Susan MacDougall
Teacher
Brick Community Primary
Learning Center
Brick, New Jersey

Jack Marine
Teacher
Raising Horizons Quest
Charter School
Philadelphia, Pennsylvania

Nicola Micozzi Jr.
Science Coordinator
Plymouth Public Schools
Plymouth, Massachusetts

Paula Monteiro
Teacher
A J Gomes Elementary
New Bedford, Massachusetts

Tracy Newallis
Teacher
Taper Avenue Elementary
San Pedro, California

Dr. Eugene Nicolo
Supervisor, Science K-12
Moorestown School District
Moorestown, New Jersey

Jeffrey Pastrak
School District of Philadelphia
Philadelphia, Pennsylvania

Helen Pedigo
Teacher
Mt. Carmel Elementary
Huntsville Alabama

Becky Peltonen
Teacher
Patterson Elementary School
Panama City, Florida

Sherri Pensler
Teacher/ESOL
Claude Pepper Elementary
Miami, Florida

Virginia Rogliano
Teacher
Bridgeview Elementary
South Charleston, West
Virginia

Debbie Sanders
Teacher
Thunderbolt Elementary
Orange Park, Florida

Grethel Santamarina
Teacher
E.W.F. Stirrup School
Miami, Florida

Migdalia Schneider
Teacher/Bilingual
Lindell School
Long Beach, New York

Susan Shelly
Teacher
Bonita Springs Elementary
Bonita Springs, Florida

Peggy Terry
Teacher
Madison District 151
South Holland, Illinois

Jane M. Thompson
Teacher
Emma Ward Elementary
Lawrenceburg, Kentucky

Martha Todd
Teacher
W. H. Rhodes Elementary
Milton, Florida

Renee Williams
Teacher
Central Elementary
Bloomfield, New Mexico

Myra Wood
Teacher
Madison Street Academy
Ocala, Florida

Marion Zampa
Teacher
Shawnee Mission
School District
Overland Park, Kansas

Science

See learning in a whole new light

Unit A Life Science

How do the different parts of a plant help it live and grow?

Chapter 1 • Plants and How They Grow

Chapter 2 • How Animals Live

How do different animals live, grow, and change?

Chapter 3 • Where Plants and Animals Live

How are ecosystems different from each other?

Chapter 4 • Plants and Animals Living Together

How do plants and animals interact?

Unit B Earth Science

How does water change form?

How does weather follow patterns?

Chapter 5 • Water

Chapter 6 • Weather

Chapter 7 • Rocks and Soil

Why are rocks and soil important resources?

Unit B Earth Science

How do forces cause changes on Earth's surface?

Chapter 8 • Changes on Earth

Chapter 9 • Natural Resources

How can people use natural resources responsibly?

Unit C   Physical Science

What are the properties of matter?

What are physical and chemical changes in matter?

Chapter 12 • Forces and Motion

How do forces cause motion and get work done?

Unit C Physical Science

How does energy change form?

Chapter 13 • Energy

Chapter 14 • Sound

How does energy produce the sounds we hear?

Unit D   Space and Technology

What patterns do the Earth, Sun, Moon, and stars show?

How are the planets in the solar system alike and different?

Chapter 15 • Patterns in the Sky

Chapter 16 • The Solar System

Chapter 17 • Science in Our Lives

How to Read Science

A page like the one below is found near the beginning of each chapter. It shows you how to use a reading skill that will help you understand what you read.

Before Reading

Before you read the chapter, read the Build Background page and think about how to answer the question. Recall what you already know as you answer the question. Work with a partner to make a list of what you already know. Then read the How to Read Science page.

Target Reading Skill
Each page has one target reading skill. The reading skill corresponds with a process skill in the Directed Inquiry activity on the facing page. The reading skill will be useful as you read science.

Real-World Connection
Each page has an example of something you might read. It also connects with the Directed Inquiry activity.

Graphic Organizer
A useful strategy for understanding anything you read is to make a graphic organizer. A graphic organizer can help you think about the information and how parts of it relate to each other. Each reading skill has a graphic organizer.

How to Read Science

Reading Skills

Compare and Contrast
When you **compare** things, you tell how they are alike. When you **contrast** things, you tell how they are different.
- Words and phrases such as *similar, like, all, both,* or *in the same way* are clues that things are being compared.
- Words and phrases such as *different, unlike,* or *in a different way* are clues that things are being contrasted.

Magazine Article

Rock Collectors
Ben and Misha both collect rocks. Ben prefers brightly colored rocks. He is a member of a rock hunters club that goes on collecting trips. Misha has a different way of collecting his favorite kinds of rocks—fossil rocks. His uncle sends Misha fossil rocks from all around the world. Unlike Ben, Misha just has to make a trip to his mailbox to add to his collection.

Apply It!
You can use a graphic organizer as a **model** to show how things compare and contrast.

Different   Alike   Different

Ben   Misha

Use a graphic organizer to show ways that Ben and Misha are alike and different in the way they collect rocks.

197

Properties of Minerals

Mineral	Color	Luster	Streak	Hardness
Mica Mica breaks into flaky pieces when struck.	black, gray, green, violet	pearly on surfaces	white	can be scratched with a knife
Molybdenite This mineral is one of the strongest and most commonly used heat-resistant metals.	silvery	metallic	bluish gray	can be scratched with a fingernail
Crocoite Much of this mineral comes from Australia.	reddish-orange	very shiny	orange-yellow	can be scratched with a coin

Another way to identify a mineral is to test its hardness. Some minerals, such as talc, are so soft you can scratch them with your fingernail. The hardest mineral is diamond. It can be scratched only by another diamond.

Some minerals can be identified by their appearance. Gold, for example, appears sometimes in nugget form. Other minerals can be identified by taste, smell, or touch.

1. ✔**Checkpoint** What are ways to identify minerals?

2. **Compare and Contrast** How are rocks and minerals alike? How are they different? Use a graphic organizer to show your answer.

203

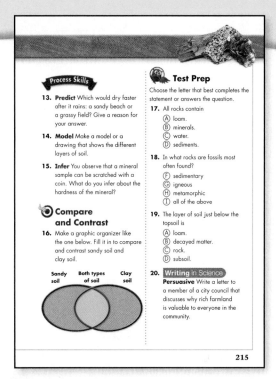

Process Skills

13. **Predict** Which would dry faster after it rains: a sandy beach or a grassy field? Give a reason for your answer.

14. **Model** Make a model or a drawing that shows the different layers of soil.

15. **Infer** You observe that a mineral sample can be scratched with a coin. What do you infer about the hardness of the mineral?

Compare and Contrast

16. Make a graphic organizer like the one below. Fill it in to compare and contrast sandy soil and clay soil.

Sandy soil   Both types of soil   Clay soil

Test Prep

Choose the letter that best completes the statement or answers the question.

17. All rocks contain
- (A) loam.
- (B) minerals.
- (C) water.
- (D) sediments.

18. In what rocks are fossils most often found?
- (F) sedimentary
- (G) igneous
- (H) metamorphic
- (I) all of the above

19. The layer of soil just below the topsoil is
- (A) loam.
- (B) decayed matter.
- (C) rock.
- (D) subsoil.

20. **Writing** in Science
Persuasive Write a letter to a member of a city council that discusses why rich farmland is valuable to everyone in the community.

215

During Reading

As you read the lesson, use the Checkpoint to check your understanding. Some checkpoints ask you to use the target reading skill.

After Reading

After you have read the chapter, think about what you found out. Exchange ideas with a partner. Compare the list you made before you read the chapter with what you learned by reading it. Answer the questions in the Chapter Review. One question uses the target reading skill.

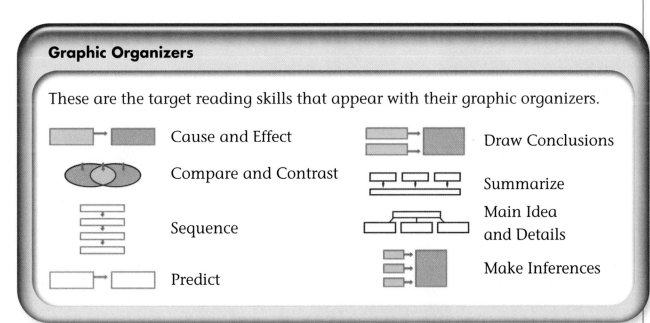

Graphic Organizers

These are the target reading skills that appear with their graphic organizers.

Cause and Effect

Compare and Contrast

Sequence

Predict

Draw Conclusions

Summarize

Main Idea and Details

Make Inferences

Science Process Skills

Investigating Weather

Scientists use process skills when they investigate places or events. You will use these skills when you do the activities in this book. Which process skills might scientists use when they investigate weather?

Observe

A scientist who studies weather observes many things. You use your senses too to find out about other objects, events, or living things.

Classify

Scientists classify clouds according to their properties. When you classify, you arrange or sort objects, events, or living things.

Estimate and Measure

Scientists estimate how much rain will fall. Then they use tools to measure how much rain fell.

Infer
Scientists infer what they think is happening during a storm, based on what they already know.

Predict
Scientists predict how weather will change. Then people know how to get ready for the change.

Make and Use Models
Scientists make and use models such as pictures and maps. Models are like real events in some ways, but are different in other ways.

Make Operational Definitions
Scientists can use what they know to make operational definitions about what they observe during a storm.

Science Process Skills

Form Questions and Hypotheses

Think of a statement that you can test to solve a problem or answer a question about storms or other kinds of weather.

Investigate and Experiment

As scientists observe storms, they investigate and experiment to test a hypothesis.

Identify and Control Variables

As scientists perform an experiment, they identify and control the variables so that they test only one thing at a time.

If you were a scientist, you might want to learn more about storms. What questions might you have about storms? How would you use process skills in your investigation?

Collect Data
Scientists collect data
from their observations
of weather. They put
the data into charts or
tables.

Interpret Data
Scientists use the
information they
collected to solve
problems or answer
questions.

Communicate
Scientists use words,
pictures, charts,
and graphs to share
information about their
investigation.

Using Scientific Methods for Science Inquiry

Scientists use scientific methods as they work. Scientific methods are organized ways to answer questions and solve problems. Scientific methods include the steps shown here. Scientists might not use all the steps. They might not use the steps in this order. You will use scientific methods when you do the **Full Inquiry** activity at the end of each unit. You also will use scientific methods when you do Science Fair Projects.

Ask a question.

You might have a question about something you observe.

What material is best for keeping heat in water?

State your hypothesis.

A hypothesis is a possible answer to your question.

If I wrap the jar in fake fur, then the water will stay warm the longest.

Identify and control variables.

Variables are things that can change. For a fair test, you choose just one variable to change. Keep all other variables the same.

Test other materials. Put the same amount of warm water in other jars that are the same size and shape.

Test your hypothesis.

Make a plan to test your hypothesis. Collect materials and tools. Then follow your plan.

Collect and record your data.

Keep good records of what you do and find out. Use tables and pictures to help.

Interpret your data.

Organize your notes and records to make them clear. Make diagrams, charts, or graphs to help.

State your conclusion.

Your conclusion is a decision you make based on your data. Communicate what you found out. Tell whether or not your data supported your hypothesis.

Fake fur kept the water warm longest. My data supported my hypothesis.

Go further.

Use what you learn. Think of new questions to test or better ways to do a test.

Ask a Question

State Your Hypothesis

Identify and Control Variables

Test Your Hypothesis

Collect and Record Your Data

Interpret Your Data

State Your Conclusion

Go Further

Science Tools

Scientists use many different kinds of tools. Tools can make objects appear larger. They can help you measure volume, temperature, length distance, and mass. Tools can help you figure out amounts and analyze your data. Tools can also help you find the latest scientific information.

You should use **safety goggles** to protect your eyes.

You use a **thermometer** to measure temperature. Many thermometers have both Fahrenheit and Celsius scales. Scientists usually use only the Celsius scale.

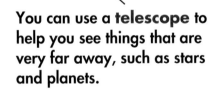

You can use a **telescope** to help you see things that are very far away, such as stars and planets.

Binoculars make far-away objects appear larger, so you can see more of their details.

A **hand lens** doesn't enlarge things as much as a microscope does, but it is easier to carry.

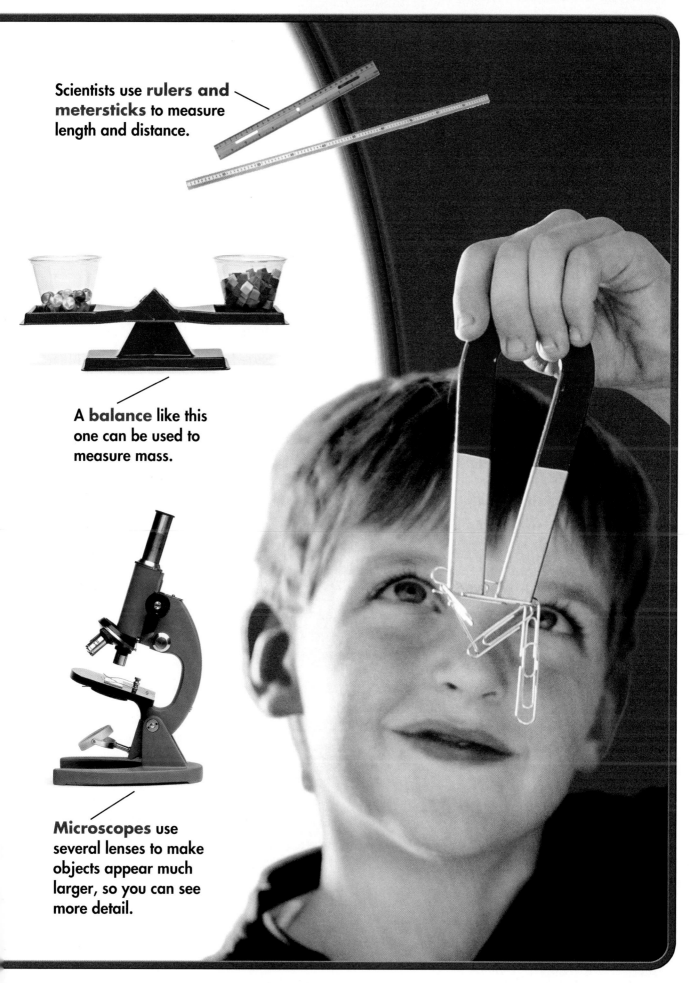

Scientists use **rulers and metersticks** to measure length and distance.

A **balance** like this one can be used to measure mass.

Microscopes use several lenses to make objects appear much larger, so you can see more detail.

Science Tools

Magnets can be used to test if an object is made of certain metals such as iron.

Pictures taken with a **camera** record what something looks like. You can compare pictures of the same object to show how the object might have changed.

A **graduated cylinder** can be used to measure volume, or the amount of space an object takes up.

Calipers can be used to measure the width of an object.

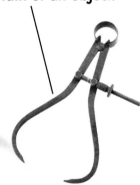

You can figure amounts using a **calculator**.

Scientists use **computers** in many ways, such as collecting, recording, and analyzing data.

You can talk into a **sound recorder** to record information you want to remember.

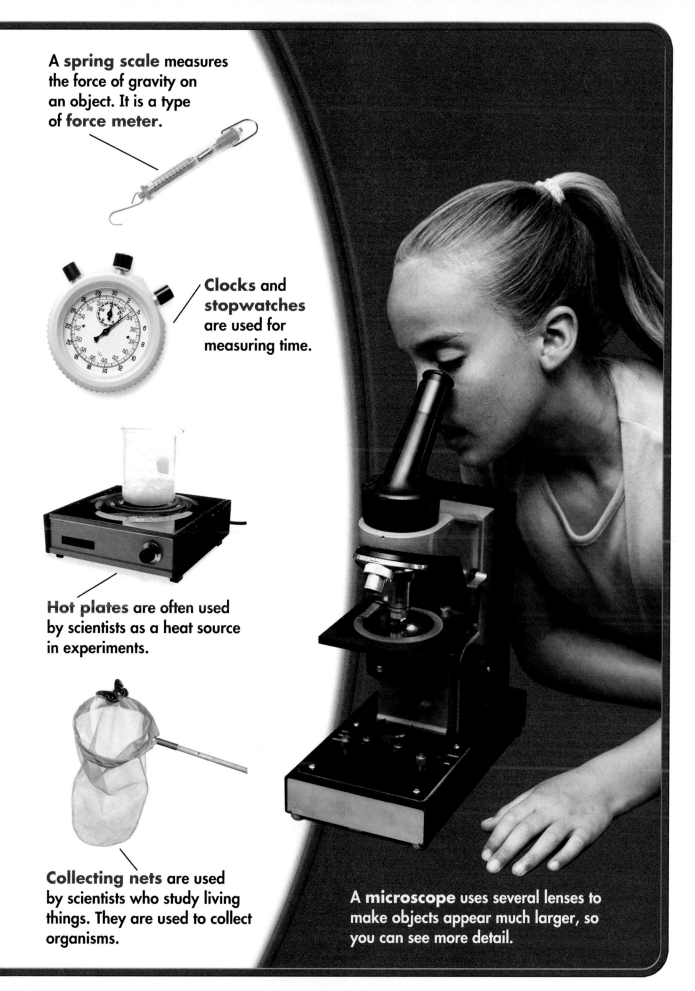

A **spring scale** measures the force of gravity on an object. It is a type of **force meter**.

Clocks and **stopwatches** are used for measuring time.

Hot plates are often used by scientists as a heat source in experiments.

Collecting nets are used by scientists who study living things. They are used to collect organisms.

A **microscope** uses several lenses to make objects appear much larger, so you can see more detail.

Safety in Science

You need to be careful when doing science activities. This page includes safety tips to remember:

- Listen to your teacher's instructions.

- Read each activity carefully.

- Never taste or smell materials unless your teacher tells you to.

- Wear safety goggles when needed.

- Handle scissors and other equipment carefully.

- Keep your work place neat and clean.

- Clean up spills immediately.

- Tell your teacher immediately about accidents or if you see something that looks unsafe.

- Wash your hands well after every activity.

- Return all materials to their proper places.

Chapter 1

Plants
and
How They Grow

You Will Discover

○ ways parts of a plant help it survive.
○ different types of plants.
○ different ways plants make more plants.
○ that plants have changed over time.

online
Student Edition
sfsuccessnet.com

1

How do the different parts of a plant help it live and grow?

system

coniferous

pollinate

seed leaf

germinate

2

deciduous

seedling

fossil

extinct

3

Explore How are plants alike and different?

Materials

grass

radish

hand lens

What to Do

1 **Observe** each plant with a hand lens. Notice the characteristics of their leaves and roots.

2 Look for the places where the leaves grow from the stems of the plants.

3 Look at the roots that grow from the stems of the plants.

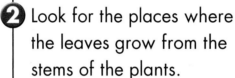

root

root

Explain Your Results

Use what you **observed** to explain how the two plants are alike and different.

How to Read Science

Compare and Contrast

Knowing how to compare and contrast can help you understand what you read and the things you **observe.**

- We **compare** when we say how things are alike. We **contrast** when we say how things are different.
- Words and phrases such as *similar, like, all, both,* or *in the same way* are used to compare.
- Words and phrases such as *unlike* or *in a different way* are used to contrast.

Science Article

Plants and Animals

Both plants and animals are living things that need food, air, water, and space to live. Unlike most plants, most animals don't stay in the same place. They move around. Unlike animals, most plants have roots that keep them in the same place.

Plants	Both	Animals
Ways that plants are different from animals	Ways that plants and animals are alike	Ways that animals are different from plants

Apply It!

Make a graphic organizer like the one shown. Use the information from the science article to fill it in.

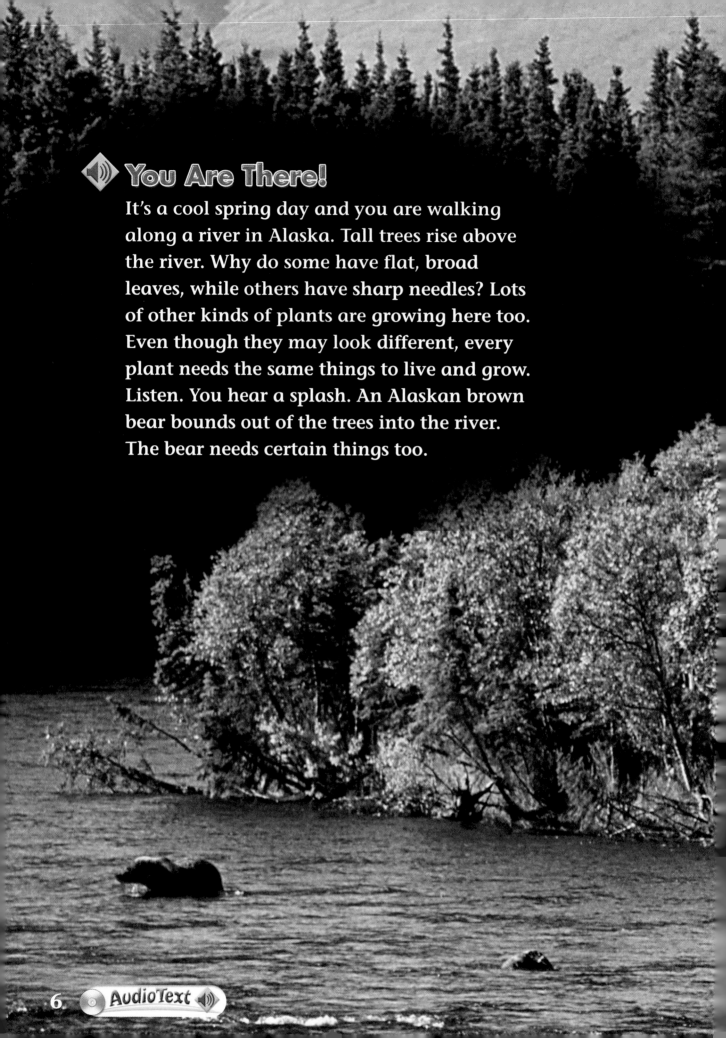

You Are There!

It's a cool spring day and you are walking along a river in Alaska. Tall trees rise above the river. Why do some have flat, broad leaves, while others have sharp needles? Lots of other kinds of plants are growing here too. Even though they may look different, every plant needs the same things to live and grow. Listen. You hear a splash. An Alaskan brown bear bounds out of the trees into the river. The bear needs certain things too.

AudioText

What are the main parts of a plant?

Most plants have four main parts. These parts are leaves, roots, stems, and flowers. In different kinds of plants, these parts may look similar. They may also look very different.

What All Living Things Need

Most living things, including plants and animals, need food, air, water, and space to live and grow. Animals find and eat plants or other animals to get their food. Unlike animals, plants can make their own food. To make their food, plants need energy from the Sun. Most plants also need soil.

Most plants have four main parts. These parts are leaves, roots, stems, and flowers.

Black-eyed Susans are one of the many plants you might see in a prairie.

1. ✓**Checkpoint** What do plants and animals need to live?

2. **Writing** in Science **Descriptive**
Choose an animal and a plant and describe in your **science journal** what each needs to survive.

7

Why Plants Need Leaves

A plant's leaves make up its leaf system. A **system** consists of parts that work together. Leaves come in many shapes and sizes. They help green plants because they make food. The food they make is a kind of sugar.

To make food, leaves use air, water, and the energy of sunlight. Carbon dioxide is a gas in air. It enters the plant through tiny holes on the underside of leaves. Water passes from soil through roots and stems and into each leaf. The leaves change the carbon dioxide and water into sugar and oxygen. Oxygen goes out from the plant through the same tiny holes on the lower surface of the leaves. The plant uses the sugar to live and grow.

Gas
Carbon dioxide enters the leaf through tiny holes on its underside.

Water
Water enters the leaf from the roots and stem.

Sugar
The leaves make sugar for food that passes through the stems to the rest of the plant.

Oxygen
Plants make and let out oxygen gas when they make sugar.

Sun
Plants need energy from the Sun to change carbon dioxide and water into sugar and oxygen.

Leaf Veins
Tiny tubes called leaf veins deliver water to the leaf. They also carry sugar made in the leaves to the rest of the plant.

Other Ways Leaves Help Plants

Leaves help plants in other ways. They help plants to balance the amount of water plants take in. If there is too much water in the plant, leaves will let some water out through the tiny holes on their underside. Plants in dry places may have leaves with waxy or fuzzy coatings to help keep water in.

A plant's leaves may also help to protect the plant from being eaten. Leaves might be poisonous, sharp, or tough to chew. Hungry animals will leave the plant alone.

✓ Lesson Checkpoint

1. List the main parts of most plants.

2. How does a leaf help a plant live?

3. **Compare and Contrast** Describe ways that leaves are alike and different. Use a graphic organizer.

Types of Leaves

Some trees have leaves that look like needles.

A pecan tree leaf is made up of many smaller leaflets that grow across from each other.

This oak leaf is more like the pecan leaves than the needle-like leaves. Yet observe how different it is.

Why do plants need roots and stems?

Along with their leaves, plants need their root and stem systems to live and grow.

How Roots Help Plants

The root system of a plant is often below the ground where you cannot see it. The roots hold the plant in the ground. Roots take in water and materials called minerals from the soil. The roots also store food made by the plant.

Many plants, such as carrots and dandelions, have a large root called a taproot. The taproot grows deep into the soil. The taproot stores food for the plant. Have you ever tasted a carrot or a beet? If your answer is "yes," then you've eaten the taproot of a plant!

A young fir tree has a tangled root system.

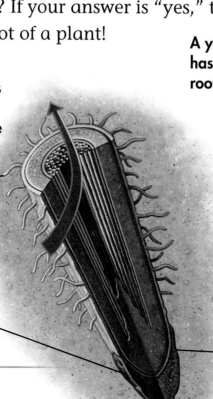

Water and minerals travel up the root through tubes to the stem and leaves.

Root hair

Water enters the root through the root hairs.

Growing tip of root

Grasses do not have a taproot.

Roots that We Eat

Beet

Radish

Carrot

Turnip

At the tips of roots are tiny root hairs. Plants take in water through their root hairs. Root branches with their many root hairs grow far into the soil to reach water. Water travels through tubes to the plant's stem and leaves.

On summer days, the root system can be a very busy place. Sunshine and hot air can dry a plant out. The roots must take in water to replace water lost from the plant leaves.

1. ✓**Checkpoint** How do roots help a plant?
2. **Social Studies in Science** Look up the many different ways that people around the world use roots.

11

How Stems Help Plants

A plant's stems hold up its leaves, flowers, and fruits. Most plant stems have tubes that move water and minerals from the roots of plants to the leaves. Other tubes carry food from the leaves of plants to the stems and roots.

The pictures show some different kinds of stems. Some stems, called stolons, are thin and grow along the surface of the ground. These stems can grow roots and a new plant. Some stems, called vines, grow parts that wrap around objects that support the plant.

Notice how thick cactus stems can be. Cactus stems swell up as they store water. The stems shrink as the plant uses water. Cactus stems also have a thick, waxy covering to help keep them from losing water. This type of stem helps the cactus plant survive in a desert.

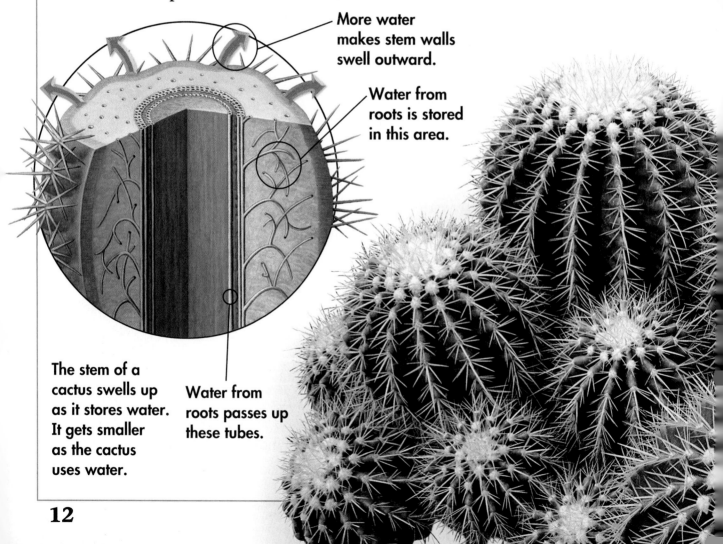

More water makes stem walls swell outward.

Water from roots is stored in this area.

The stem of a cactus swells up as it stores water. It gets smaller as the cactus uses water.

Water from roots passes up these tubes.

12

Stolons of this strawberry plant are for growing new plants.

Potato

Parts of some stems grow underground. When you eat a potato, you eat a stem part that stored food underground. Underground stems can sprout new stems from buds such as the potato's "eyes." These parts grow upward and become new plants.

Vine

Some plants have stems with special features to help them survive. For example, some stems have thorns, spines, or stinging hairs to keep hungry animals from eating them.

The spines growing out of this cactus stem are a special kind of leaf.

Tree trunk

✓ Lesson Checkpoint

1. How do stems help a plant?

2. How are roots and stems alike and different?

3. **Writing** in Science **Expository**
Write a paragraph in your **science journal** that describes the special features of a cactus. Explain how these features help the cactus.

How are plants grouped?

Plants can be grouped by the kinds of parts they have.

Flowering Plants

An apple tree, a grass, and a cactus are flowering plants but each is in a different group. Plants in each group have different kinds of roots, stems, leaves, and flowers. Look at the examples below. Both plants grow flowers with seeds. But the dogwood tree can grow tall with the help of a stiff, woody stem. Many flowering plants, such as grasses and the trillium below, do not have wood. They grow low to the ground.

The dogwood tree survives winter because its leaves die and fall off in the fall. The tree then grows new leaves in the spring. Trees that lose their leaves are **deciduous.** The dogwood tree is a deciduous tree. Many grasses and plants like the trillium die all the way down to the roots instead. In the spring, they grow back again from the roots.

Flowering trees and small flowering plants are similar and different.

Making Seeds

Flowering plants grow flowers that make seeds. Flowers have parts that make pollen or seeds. Bees, other animals, or wind **pollinate** a flower when they move pollen to the flower part that makes seeds.

After a flower is pollinated, seeds form near the center of the flower. A fruit often grows to surround and protect the seeds.

A flower's petals attract insects and other animals that pollinate the flower.

Pollen sticks to the bodies of bees as bees look for food. They carry this pollen to the part of the flower that makes seeds.

The tip of this part of the flower makes pollen.

Pollen put on the tip of this part helps form seeds down here.

1. ✓**Checkpoint** Describe how a flower makes a seed.

2. **Writing in Science** **Narrative** Write a story in your **science journal** about a flower that invited a bee over for a visit. Be sure to describe the bee's thank-you gift.

Coniferous Trees

Coniferous trees do not lose all their leaves in the fall. The leaves of coniferous trees look like needles or brushes. These trees also grow cones instead of flowers to make their seeds. Coniferous trees include pine, fir, spruce, and hemlock.

Two Types of Cones

Coniferous trees make two kinds of cones. They make small pollen cones and large seed cones. Wind blows pollen from the small pollen cones to the large seed cones. When pollen attaches to the seed cone, seeds begin to grow. A seed grows under each scale of the seed cone. When the seeds are ripe, they fall to the ground. If conditions are right, each seed can start growing into a new plant. Over time, the seeds may become trees.

16

Cones form on branches near the top of conifers.

Wind blows pollen from these small cones to larger cones on other trees.

Seeds are made under the scales of this Douglas fir cone. This cone is about as big as your fist.

Larger cones grow with seeds inside.

✓ Lesson Checkpoint

1. What are two ways to group plants?

2. Describe two kinds of plant parts that can make seeds.

3. **Writing** in Science **Expository** Write a paragraph in your **science journal** that explains different ways flowers can be pollinated.

Coniferous seeds glide to the ground.

How do new plants grow?

Most plants make seeds that grow into new plants.
Sometimes a stem or root grows a new plant.

Scattering Seeds

When seeds are scattered, they are moved away
from the plant. Then they have more room to grow.

Seeds are scattered in many ways. Some seeds are spread
from one place to another by wind or water. Other seeds are
carried to new places by animals that eat fruit with seeds.
The seeds pass through the animal's body. Then they are
dropped to the ground far from the plant. Some seeds
are carried along when they stick to an animal's fur.

Ways That Seeds Scatter

Wind		Wind scatters seeds that have parachutes or wings.
Water		Water scatters seeds that float, such as coconuts.
Carried by animals		Animals scatter seeds that can stick to fur.
Eaten by animals		Animals scatter seeds when they eat fruit.

You've probably seen seeds drifting through the air. Wind scatters seeds that are very light. Many of these seeds have special parts that act like tiny wings or parachutes. The seeds can drift for long distances if the wind is strong.

Special Ways of Releasing Seeds

Some types of pine cones need to be heated in a forest fire to release their seeds. The fire also removes other plants around the trees and clears space for the seeds to grow.

Each of these seeds has a tiny parachute. Wind can carry these seeds long distances where they can grow into new plants.

1. ✓ **Checkpoint** What are two ways that animals scatter seeds?

2. **Art** in Science Draw pictures of two groups of seeds. Draw one group of seeds that are scattered by animals. Draw another group of seeds that are scattered by wind. Describe how the parts of these seeds are different.

Germinating and Growing

Seeds come in many different shapes, sizes, and colors. But they all have the same parts. Every seed has a tiny plant inside it that can grow into a new plant. Every seed also has a seed coat to protect the young plant inside the seed. And, finally, every seed has either one **seed leaf** or two seed leaves to provide food for a sprouting new plant.

Seeds need certain things to start to grow, or **germinate.** They need the right temperature, the right amount of water, and air. When conditions are right, a seed begins to sprout and a root grows from it. The seed then breaks open and a young plant, or **seedling,** begins to grow. The seedling uses food stored in the seed to grow.

As it grows, the seedling's stem rises out of the soil and grows leaves. The seedling's leaves use sunlight to make sugar for food. Soon the seedling grows into an adult plant that has flowers. The flowers are pollinated and new seeds are formed. If the seeds germinate, they grow into new plants. Then the cycle begins again.

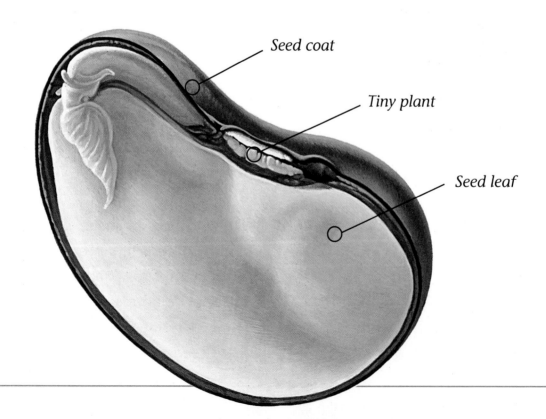

Seed coat

Tiny plant

Seed leaf

Life Cycle of a Plant

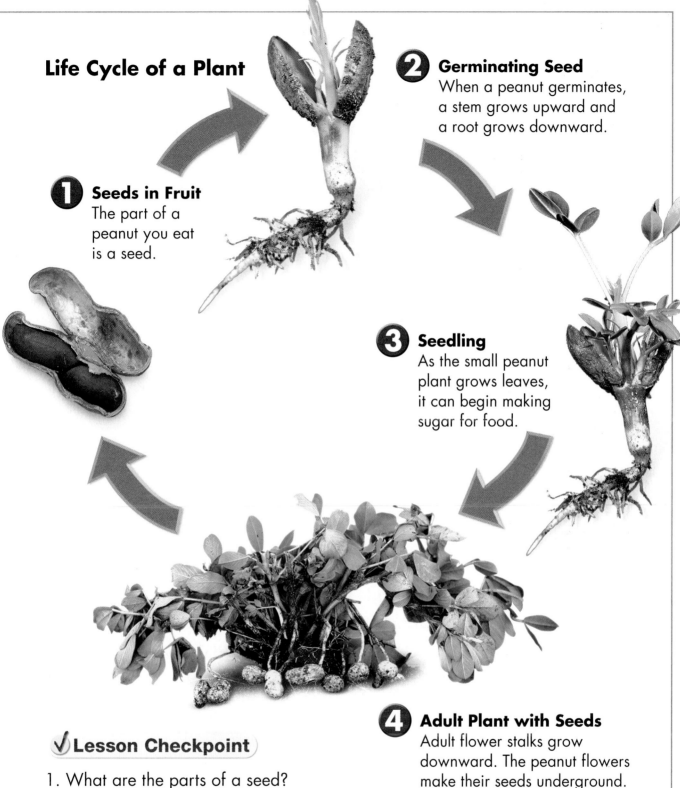

1 **Seeds in Fruit**
The part of a peanut you eat is a seed.

2 **Germinating Seed**
When a peanut germinates, a stem grows upward and a root grows downward.

3 **Seedling**
As the small peanut plant grows leaves, it can begin making sugar for food.

4 **Adult Plant with Seeds**
Adult flower stalks grow downward. The peanut flowers make their seeds underground. When the adult plant dies, it becomes part of the soil.

✓ Lesson Checkpoint

1. What are the parts of a seed?

2. Describe the life cycle of a plant starting with a seed being planted.

3. **Social Studies** in Science   Choose a vegetable that is grown in your state. Find out what farmers do to grow the vegetable and get it to market.

How are plants from the past like today's plants?

Fossils show the kinds of plants that lived long ago. In some ways today's plants are similar to plants from the past that have disappeared.

Plants That Lived Long Ago

We learn about plants that lived long ago by studying fossils. A **fossil** is the remains or mark of a living thing from long ago.

Look at the fern and horsetail fossils in the pictures on page 23. How did they form? Each plant died and was pressed into mud. Next, the plant rotted away. But the mud kept the form of the plant. Over time the mud hardened into rock. The flat imprint of the plant is seen when the rock cracks open.

Another kind of fossil is made when rock replaces the parts that make up a plant. The drawings below show how it might have formed. This rock is called a petrified fossil.

Formation of Petrified Wood

Stump is buried in mud.

Minerals replace wood as time passes.

Rock surrounding the fossil is removed.

Plant Fossils

The fern that made this fossil lived about 350 million years ago.

This fossil shows a kind of fern that is extinct.

The fossil of this horsetail shows a plant that is extinct.

This log is a fossil trunk of an extinct tree fern.

Petrified wood can form when trees are buried in the ground. Minerals replace wood in the trees. At the same time, water breaks down the wood and carries it away. Over a long period of time, the wood becomes stone with exactly the same shape and markings as the original wood.

Many kinds of plants that lived long ago are no longer alive. They are **extinct.** For example, ferns that live today look different from the ferns that lived long ago. Plants related to the extinct ferns and horsetail fossils shown in the photos live on Earth today.

1. ✓**Checkpoint** What can scientists learn by studying fossils?

2. **Writing in Science** **Expository** In your **science journal**, write a paragraph that explains how a plant leaf can become a fossil.

These petrified wood fossils in Arizona look like wood, but they are made of rock.

Plants Change Over Time

Plant fossils tell us that the first plants did not have flowers or cones. Many were like today's ferns and horsetails. As Earth changed over time, however, plants changed too. Trees that made cones appeared. Then plants with flowers appeared. Many of these kinds of plants have completely disappeared.

Magnolias are an example of a group of flowering plants that has survived. The world was warm and wet year-round when magnolias first appeared. Dinosaurs were everywhere. Big flowers dotted the branches for months. Magnolias grew thick leaves that they kept year-round. Magnolias just like this are alive today. The flower of the magnolia has remained unchanged for 100 million years.

As forms of life continued to change, so did the magnolias. Some magnolias now are deciduous. They lose their leaves in fall. Their flowers grow all at once before the leaves appear in the spring. Even so, their leaves and flowers are similar to those of magnolias that lived long ago.

Fossils of magnolia leaves from long ago look similar to today's magnolia leaves.

Flowers of deciduous magnolias grow all at once in the spring. After flowering, the trees grow new leaves for the summer.

The first magnolia trees were similar to many magnolias alive today. The feathered dinosaur is extinct.

✔️ Lesson Checkpoint

1. What is an extinct plant?

2. How do scientists learn about plants that are extinct?

3. **Compare and Contrast** How are extinct magnolias alike and different from magnolias alive today? Use a graphic organizer to show your answer.

Lab zone Guided Inquiry

Investigate How fast do different kinds of seeds germinate?

Seeds from some kinds of plants germinate faster than seeds from other kinds of plants. Even seeds from just one kind of plant may germinate faster than other seeds from the same kind of plant.

Materials

paper towel and paper plate

waxed paper and masking tape

5 radish seeds

5 corn seeds

5 pinto bean seeds

5 sunflower seeds

cup with water

metric ruler

Process Skills

By **interpreting the data** you **collected** in your chart, you can analyze how different seeds grow.

What to Do

1 Fold a paper towel in half. Fold it again.

2 Make 2 lines to divide the folded towel into 4 parts. Label each part.

3 Put the waxed paper on the plate. Put the folded towel on the waxed paper. Put on the seeds. Wet the towel.

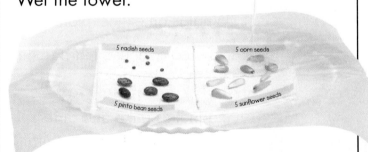

26 More Lab zone Activities Take It to the Net sfsuccessnet.com

4 Put the plate in a warm, bright place.

5 **Observe** and record changes for 1 week. Describe or draw the plants as they begin to grow and develop.

After the first day, keep the paper towels moist, but not wet.

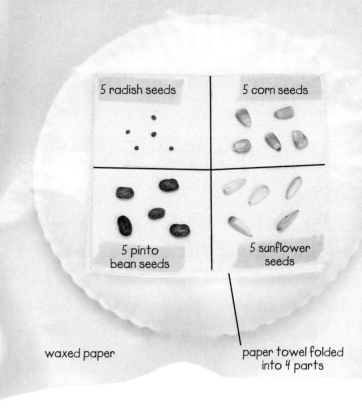

5 radish seeds

5 corn seeds

5 pinto bean seeds

5 sunflower seeds

waxed paper

paper towel folded into 4 parts

Kind of Plant	Description (write or draw)	Day the First of the 5 Seeds Germinated (Day 1, 2, 3, 4, or 5)	Order in Which Different Kinds of Plants Germinated (1st, 2nd, 3rd, or 4th)	Length of Longest Stem on Day 7 (mm)
Radish				
Corn				
Pinto				
Sunflower				

Explain Your Results

1. **Interpret the data** you **collected**. Compare the radish and sunflower seeds. How did they grow and develop differently?
2. Were all the radish plants the same? Explain.

Go Further

Collect more data. Every day count and record the number of each kind of plant that has germinated. Graph your results.

Elapsed Time
from Seed to Fruit

If you plant a green bean seed, how soon can you eat green beans from the plant that grows? The answer is the length of time it takes for the seed to germinate, grow, and produce flowers and fruit. Different kinds of plants have different lengths of time from seed to fruit that is ready to eat.

Green bean

Cucumber

Sweet corn

Tomato

eTools Take It to the Net
sfsuccessnet.com

If you plant green bean seeds on May 10, you can start eating green beans 58 days later, on July 7.

Days from planting seeds or seedling to picking ripe fruit	
green bean seeds	58 days
cucumber seeds	55 days
sweet corn seeds	75 days
tomato seedling	59 days

Use the table and calendars to answer the questions.

1 If you plant cucumber seeds on May 21, when could you start eating cucumbers?

2 If sweet corn seeds are planted on May 19, when will the corn be ready to eat?

3 When could you start eating ripe tomatoes if the seedling was planted on May 31?

Lab zone Take-Home Activity

Look at the back of seed packets or go to the library or Internet to search for seed catalogs. Find out how long it takes different kinds of seeds to grow and make fruit. Use a calendar to find what dates the fruit might be ready to pick.

Chapter 1 Review and Test Prep

Use Vocabulary

deciduous (page 14)

pollinate (page 15)

coniferous (page 16)

seed leaf (page 20)

extinct (page 23)

seedling (page 20)

fossil (page 22)

system (page 8)

germinate (page 20)

Use the vocabulary word or words from the list above that best completes each sentence.

1. When conditions are right, a seed will start to grow, or _____.

2. A tree that makes cones is a(n) _____ tree.

3. Bees, wind, and water can _____ flowers.

4. All the leaves and their parts make up a plant's leaf _____.

5. A(n) _____ tree loses all its leaves in the fall.

6. A new plant that has just grown out of the soil is a(n) _____.

7. A new plant uses food stored in a(n) _____.

8. A(n) _____ plant no longer lives on Earth, but a(n) _____ of its remains might be found.

Explain Concepts

9. How do scientists learn about plants that are extinct?

10. Explain why all of a plant's roots and their parts are called a system.

11. What do a plant's leaves need to make sugar?

Process Skills

12. **Classify** Choose one way that plants can be sorted into two groups. Explain how the plants in the two groups are alike and different.

13. **Infer** Bees visit the flowers on apple trees to get food. How might a disease that kills bees affect the number of apples the trees make? Explain your answer.

Compare and Contrast

14. Make a graphic organizer like the one shown below. Fill in the correct information.

Plants   Both   Animals

Stay in same place, make own food

Move around, find food

Test Prep

Choose the letter that best completes the statement or answers the question.

15. Before a seed can become a plant, the seed must

Ⓐ germinate.
Ⓑ be pollinated.
Ⓒ make food.
Ⓓ flower.

16. A cactus stores the most water in its

Ⓕ roots.
Ⓖ leaves.
Ⓗ stems.
Ⓘ flowers.

17. What fossil is made when minerals replace plant parts, while water breaks the parts down and carries them away?

Ⓐ imprint
Ⓑ petrified wood
Ⓒ extinct fern
Ⓓ magnolia flower

18. Which of the following is an example of scattering seeds?

Ⓕ pollen sticking to a bee
Ⓖ wind blowing pollen
Ⓗ apples growing on a tree
Ⓘ burs sticking to a dog's fur

19. Explain why the answer you chose for Question 18 is best. For each of the answers you did not choose, give a reason why it is not the best choice.

20. **Writing** in Science

Expository Write a paragraph that describes the life cycle of a plant.

Plant Researcher

Do you like plants? Plant researchers study how plants live and grow.

What if food that astronauts need during long space missions runs out? Grow more aboard ship! Dr. Stutte of NASA tests ways to grow wheat aboard the International Space Station. He also tests the ability of plants to clean the air and water that astronauts use.

Growing plants in space is tricky, however. When seeds germinate on Earth roots grow down and stems grow up. In space, there is no up or down. As a plant researcher you might be called upon to solve problems like this one.

Plant researchers look for ways to grow more or stronger plants. Researchers at NASA are studying how plant seeds might grow better in space. Better traits from seeds grown in space could help farmers grow stronger plants on Earth.

Plant researchers have college degrees.

Dr. Gary Stutte

Lab zone Take-Home Activity

Draw a machine that would grow cucumbers in space where there is little gravity. Label the parts that supply the plants with water, fertilizer, carbon dioxide, and light. Write a paragraph explaining how it would work.

Chapter 2

How Animals Live

You Will Discover

- ways that animals are grouped.
- how an animal's body and its behavior help it survive.
- how animals grow and change.
- that many animals today resemble animals that lived long ago.

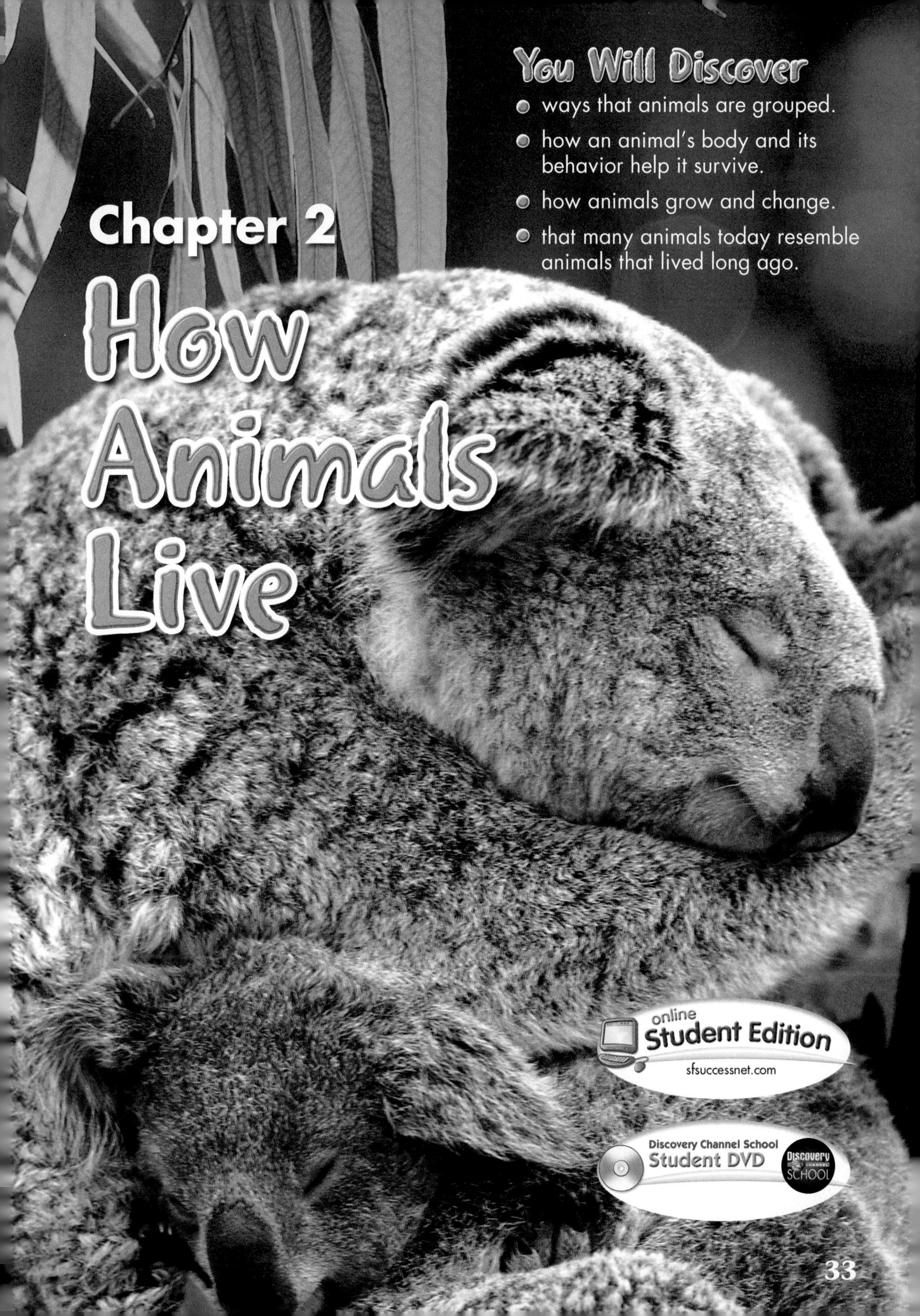

online Student Edition
sfsuccessnet.com

Discovery Channel School Student DVD

How do different animals live, grow, and change?

vertebrate

trait

inherited

migrate

hibernate

34

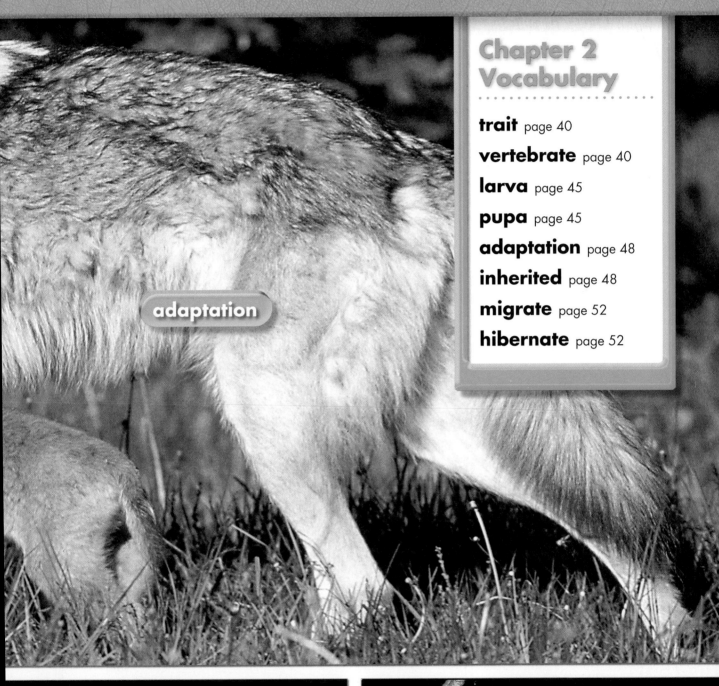

adaptation

larva

pupa

35

Explore How can you make a model of a backbone?

Materials

pipe cleaner

10 pieces of wagon wheel pasta

9 soft fruit jelly rings

What to Do

❶ **Make a model** of a backbone. Bend the end of a pipe cleaner into a knot. String a piece of wagon wheel pasta on the pipe cleaner so the pasta rests on the knot. Next string a jelly ring.

❷ Add another wheel and a ring. Keep going until you have used 10 wheels and 9 rings.

❸ Bend the other end of the pipe cleaner. Make a knot to hold everything on. Can you bend your model backbone?

Process Skills

Making and using a model can help you understand scientific ideas.

Explain Your Results

How is your **model** different from a real backbone? How is your model like a real backbone?

Sequence

Sequence is the order in which events take place. Clue words such as *first, next, then,* and *finally* can help you figure out the **sequence** of events. They are marked on the museum display card.

Museum Display Card

Sea Jelly

A sea jelly grows up in stages. First, an adult makes young called larvae. Next, each larva becomes attached to a rock. Then, each larva grows and becomes a polyp. Finally, each polyp grows into a group of young adults.

Apply It!

Make a graphic organizer as a **model** to show the life cycle of the sea jelly. Write each of the four events in the life cycle after your four clue words.

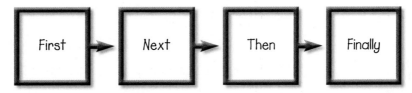

First → Next → Then → Finally

You Are There!

It's early morning in the forest and the birds are singing. You look down at your feet and notice ants marching by. You stand very still, listening and watching. Suddenly, you spot what looks like two dogs walking through a grassy field in the distance. As you focus your eyes you realize they are not dogs. You've spotted a wolf and her pup! Animals come in many shapes and sizes. Even though they may be different, do animals need the same basic things to live?

Lesson 1

How are animals grouped?

All animals have the same basic needs. Animals might be grouped by how they look, where they live, or how they act.

What All Animals Need

Nearly all animals need water, oxygen, food, and shelter to live. Animals can get water from drinking or from the foods they eat. All animals also need the gas oxygen. They get oxygen from the air or from water. Most animals that live on land have lungs to breathe in oxygen. Many animals that live in water, such as fish, breathe with gills.

Animals also need food and shelter. They get their food by eating plants or other animals. Shelters protect animals from the weather and from other animals. While some animals build or seek shelters, others use their own hard shells as their homes.

Needs of Animals

Water	Oxygen	Food	Shelter

1. ✓**Checkpoint** What do all animals need?

2. **Writing** in Science **Descriptive** In your **science journal,** write about how your favorite animal meets its basic needs.

Ways of Grouping Animals

How we group animals depends on what we want to learn about them. Sometimes animals are grouped by where they live or how they act. They also may be grouped by how they look. A body feature passed on to an animal from its parents is called a **trait.** Traits sometimes include things an animal does.

One animal might be placed into different groups. For example, a group of animals that eat mice can include snakes, hawks, and owls. A group of animals that fly would also include hawks and owls, but not snakes.

Animals with Backbones

Another way to group animals is by whether or not they have a backbone. An animal with a backbone is called a **vertebrate.** Cats, dogs, and birds are vertebrates. So are fish and snakes. Even though all these animals look very different, each one has a backbone. And that backbone grows as the animal grows.

This lynx is
a vertebrate.

Groups of Vertebrates

Fish
These vertebrates spend their entire lives in fresh water, ocean water, or both. Most fish have slippery scales and breathe through gills.

Amphibians
Frogs, toads, and salamanders belong to a group called amphibians. Many amphibians spend part of their lives in water and part on land. Most young amphibians live in water. They get oxygen through gills and through their smooth, moist skin. As they grow, most amphibians develop lungs that they use to breathe air.

Reptiles
Snakes, lizards, turtles, crocodiles, and alligators are reptiles. They mostly have dry, scaly skin. These vertebrates breathe air through lungs.

Birds
Birds are vertebrates with feathers and bills that do not have teeth. They breathe air through lungs. Wings and light bones help most birds fly. Their coats of feathers help them stay warm.

Mammals
The vertebrates that you probably know best are called mammals. Mammals have hair at least during part of their lives. The hair keeps them warm. Mammals breathe air through lungs and feed milk to their young.

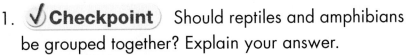

1. ✓ **Checkpoint** Should reptiles and amphibians be grouped together? Explain your answer.

2. **Art** in **Science** Think about two animals that share some of the same traits. Draw a picture of each animal "in action" using a shared trait.

Animals Without Backbones

In addition to a backbone, vertebrates also have other bones. Their bones give them strong support for their bodies. This allows many vertebrates, such as elephants, to be very big.

Most animals, however, do not have skeletons made of bone inside their bodies. These are the animals without backbones, or invertebrates. Examples include sea stars, butterflies, and spiders.

A soft sac filled with liquid supports worms and sea jellies. A hard shell supports clams and lobsters. These structures would be bulky and weigh too much on big animals. For this reason invertebrates do not get as big as vertebrates can get.

It's hard sometimes to notice invertebrates because they usually are so small. But invertebrates are everywhere on Earth. In fact, there are many more invertebrates than vertebrates. For instance, several million roundworms, each too tiny to see, may live under a square yard of soil. There are also many more kinds of invertebrates than vertebrates, as the chart at the top of the page shows.

Kinds of Animals

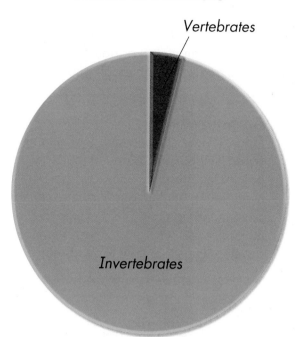

The whole circle stands for all kinds of animals. The small piece shows that kinds of vertebrates are only a small part of the total.

Kinds of Invertebrate Animals

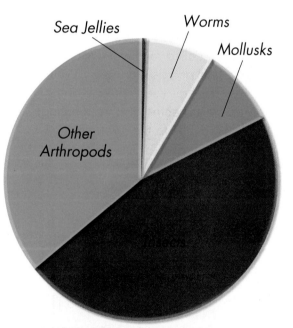

Most kinds of invertebrates are insects.

Major Kinds of Invertebrate Animals

Sea Jellies	Sea jellies have soft bodies and long, stinging body parts. The body of a sea jelly is made mostly of water. A sea jelly uses its stingers to stun its prey before pulling it into its stomach. Most sea jellies live in the ocean.	
Worms	Worms are animals with long, soft bodies and no legs. You've probably seen an earthworm in the soil. These invertebrates help keep soil healthy.	
Mollusks	Mollusks are animals with soft bodies. Some mollusks include the octopus, squid, clam, and snail. Many mollusks have a hard shell.	
Arthropods	These animals are members of the largest group of invertebrates. They wear their skeletons outside their bodies. The bodies of arthropods are made up of more than one main part and they have legs with joints. Insects, spiders, and crabs are all arthropods.	

✓ Lesson Checkpoint

1. If a rattlesnake and a black widow spider both make poison, why are they put in different groups?

2. Explain why most invertebrates are small in size compared to most vertebrates.

3. **Math in Science** There are 5 vertebrates in someone's backyard. There are 20 times as many invertebrates as vertebrates there, too. How many invertebrates are there?

How do animals grow and change?

Different animals have their young in different ways. But all animals grow and change during their life cycle.

Life Cycles

An animal's life starts out as an egg. Sometimes the egg develops into a young animal inside the mother. Then the mother gives birth to a live young. For other animals, the mother lays an egg outside of her body. Then the young develops in the egg and hatches when it is ready.

When some animals hatch or are born, they look like their parents. Many other animals change a lot before they look anything like their parents.

Adult butterflies lay eggs.

Life Cycle Stages	
Birth	Animals are born or hatch.
Growth	Animals get bigger.
Development	Animals change into adults.
Reproduction	Animals produce young.
Death	Animals' lives come to an end.

1 **Egg**
This is a close-up view of a very small egg. The picture has been magnified, or made to look bigger.

4 Butterfly
The adult butterfly comes out of the chrysalis.

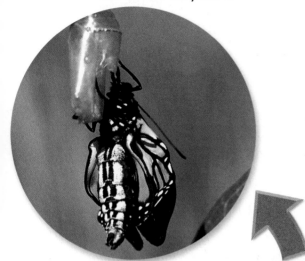

3 Pupa
Inside a hard covering, the larva's body changes.

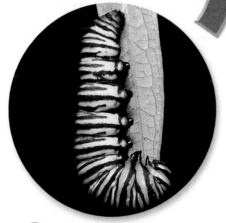

2 Larva
The butterfly larva is called a caterpillar.

A Butterfly's Life Cycle

The butterfly's life begins in an egg so tiny it is hard to see.

A caterpillar hatches from the egg, the first stage in its life cycle. It is now a **larva.** In order to survive and continue in its life cycle, the caterpillar must eat a lot. It starts munching on the plant where it lives.

As the caterpillar grows, it sheds its skin several times. Then the larva spins a covering around itself. Then a hard covering, or chrysalis, forms. The larva is now called a **pupa.** The caterpillar's body changes a lot while a pupa. It grows wings and jointed legs. It finally begins to look like an adult butterfly. Soon it breaks out of the chrysalis and crawls out. The adult butterfly dries its wings and flies away. After laying eggs, the butterfly's life cycle is nearly complete. It will soon die, the last stage in its life cycle.

1. ✔**Checkpoint** What is the purpose of the pupa?

2. **Sequence** List the sequence of steps in a butterfly's life cycle. Use the signal words *first, next, then,* and *finally.*

Some Vertebrate Life Cycles

Vertebrates have different kinds of life cycles. Some vertebrates, like frogs, go through many changes as they grow and mature. Other vertebrates, like pandas or monkeys, do not change as much.

A Frog's Life Cycle

Just like insects, many amphibians change quite a lot as they become adults. Did you know, for instance, that a very young frog looks and acts a lot like a fish?

Look at how a frog changes during its life cycle. This frog completes all the stages of its life cycle in one summer. All frogs do not develop in the same way. In colder places, a developing frog may dig into the mud during the winter. It will not become an adult frog until the following spring or summer.

A panda cub gets a gentle nudge.

Even though it's very small, a new-born panda pup has the same body form and the same number of legs as its parents.

A Mammal's Life Cycle

Unlike amphibians and insects, young mammals do not change very much as they become adults. Many mammals look like their parents when they are born. Like you, they grow as they get older.

Most mammals develop inside their mother's bodies. When they are born, the babies drink milk from their mothers. They also have hair or fur.

It will be many years before you become an adult. A young rabbit, however, is ready to leave its nest and live on its own when it is less than three weeks old. It will be an adult at about six months.

Frog Life Cycle

② Tadpole
Tadpoles hatch from the frog eggs. Tadpoles live underwater and breathe with gills.

① Eggs
Mother frogs often lay hundreds or thousands of eggs in the water.

③ Growing Tadpole
As the tadpole grows, it starts to change. Its tail becomes shorter. Legs begin to grow. The back legs grow first.

Before a tadpole becomes an adult frog, it has to grow lungs so it can breathe on land.

④ Adult Frog
The adult frog lives on land and in the water. It will need to return to the water to lay its eggs.

✓ Lesson Checkpoint

1. Before a frog can live on land, how must its body change?

2. How is a mammal's life cycle different from a frog's or a butterfly's life cycle?

3. **Writing in Science** **Expository** Think about how mammals care for their young. In your **science journal,** describe why this kind of care might be helpful for most mammals.

Lesson 3

How do adaptations help animals?

Animals have special body parts, features, and ways of doing things that help them survive in their environments.

Adaptations

Animals live in many different places on Earth. An animal needs food, water, oxygen, and shelter. A trait that helps an animal meet its needs in the place where it lives is called an **adaptation.**

The webbed feet of a pelican are an adaptation. They help the pelican swim and survive in the water where it finds its food. Adaptations, such as webbed feet, are **inherited,** or passed on, from parents to their young.

Body parts, such as feet and bills, are important inherited adaptations. There are many different kinds of adaptations. Most kinds, such as body color, differ between members of even closely related groups.

This porcupine skull shows adaptations of a plant-eating animal. Sharp front teeth cut off parts of plants. Flat teeth in the back of the jaw move from side to side, grinding tough plant material.

This hyena skull shows adaptations of a meat-eating animal. Sharp front teeth tear off meat and back teeth shred it.

48

The bill of a pelican has a pouch that hangs from it. When a pelican swoops into the water for food, the pouch acts like a net to help the bird catch fish.

Adaptations for Getting Food

Animals have many special adaptations for getting food. Prairie dogs and moles have feet that are especially good for digging. Hawks and eagles have feet that can hold tightly onto their food when they swoop down to catch it. Animals may also have the kind of teeth that can handle the foods they eat. Many birds have bills that help them catch and eat their favorite foods. Sometimes you can tell what a bird eats by the shape of its bill.

A long, curved bill helps the flamingo filter food from shallow water.

A short, strong bill helps the cardinal break open seeds.

A small, thin bill helps the warbler pick out insects for food.

1. ✓ Checkpoint Give two examples of adaptations and tell how they help the animal survive.

2. Art in Science Think about an animal that wades into ponds and spears fish for food. Draw a picture of this animal. Include the special adaptations you think it would need to live and get food.

Adaptations for Protection

The way an animal looks and the way it acts can help it survive. Some animals protect themselves by blending into their surroundings so they are hard to spot. This is called *camouflage*. Other animals protect themselves by looking like a dangerous or poisonous animal. This adaptation is called *mimicry*. The animals mimic or copy another animal. The animal being copied is usually more dangerous. Many animals will climb, run, hop, jump, fly, or swim away from danger.

Animals may also use poison to protect themselves. Animals such as skunks and weasels will spray a bad odor at their enemies. Special body parts such as shells, teeth, claws, hooves, bills, or pointed body parts also protect animals from danger.

For example, the porcupine is covered in quills. These special hairs have sharp hooks on their tips. When the porcupine is scared or threatened, it uses special muscles to make the quills stand up. Then it turns around and swings its tail. If the porcupine hits an attacker with its tail, the quills can let go as they pierce the attacker's skin. The hooks on the quills keep them attached to the attacker.

Porcupines have loose, barbed quills to protect them from their enemies.

Ways Animals Protect Themselves

Camouflage	Armor	Mimicry	Poison
Animals that can harm or be harmed by this crab spider cannot see it.	Spikes and horns protect this horned lizard.	A harmless hover fly looks like a dangerous hornet.	Lion fish have poisonous spines.
These harlequin shrimp blend in with the bright sea fans.	Pill bugs roll into a ball for defense.	A viceroy butterfly looks like a bad-tasting monarch butterfly.	Monarch butterflies taste bad because of the food they eat.
The fur color of this arctic fox changes with the seasons.	A cassowary has a tough helmet to protect its head as it runs through brush.	This king snake looks similar to the deadly coral snake.	Coral snakes bite with poisonous fangs.

1. ✓**Checkpoint** What are some ways that animals protect themselves from their enemies?

2. **Sequence** List in the correct sequence what happens when a predator attacks a porcupine. Be sure to use the signal words *first, next,* and *finally* in your list of steps.

Behaviors That Help Animals

Behaviors are things that animals do. Animals are born being able to do some things. These behaviors are inherited. You inherit your ability to do many things such as walk and talk.

You do not inherit your ability to read and write. You need to learn these behaviors. You do inherit your ability to learn these behaviors, though.

Baby birds are born knowing how to open their mouths for food.

Monarch butterflies have an instinct to migrate.

Instincts

An instinct is a behavior an animal is born able to do. One instinct is an animal's response to hunger. Baby birds, for example, open their mouths when they sense a parent with food is near. Some animals have an instinct to move, or **migrate,** when the seasons change. Some butterflies migrate thousands of miles to warmer weather to survive the winter.

Other animals have an instinct to **hibernate** during the cold winter months. When animals hibernate, their body systems usually slow down to save energy. Then they don't need as much food to survive.

Bats hibernate during the winter months when food is hard to find.

An adult chimp shows a young chimp how to dig for insects.

Learning

Animals learn some behaviors from their parents and other animals. For example, chimpanzees can learn how to use tools like sticks to catch insects to eat. Chimpanzees are not born knowing how to use sticks as tools. They learn how to do this by watching other chimpanzees. Young chimpanzees also learn which foods are safe to eat from their mothers and other adults.

Some young animals learn hunting behavior from their parents.

✔ Lesson Checkpoint

1. Name two types of adaptations having to do with an animal's actions.

2. Why do some animals migrate or hibernate?

3. **Social Studies** in Science
   Chimpanzees live in groups and learn how to behave from other chimpanzees. Describe how humans and chimpanzees are alike in the ways that they learn.

53

This trilobite fossil is a cast. It shows what the trilobite looked like.

A cast, such as this bird-like dinosaur, is in the shape of the original fossil. It formed when a mold was filled in with rock matter over time.

This fossil cast is of a dinosaur skull about 125 million years old! It looks like the skull of a modern-day crocodile.

How are animals from the past like today's animals?

Fossils show the kinds of animals that lived long ago. Today's animals are similar in some ways to animals of the past that have disappeared.

Animals That Lived Long Ago

Signs of past life are called fossils. Usually only the hard parts of animals become fossils. A fossil is usually not the actual bone or part. Instead, it is rock in the shape of the part.

A space in the shape of an animal in rock is called a fossil mold. Soft earth covers the remains of the animal, which wears away. This leaves a cavity or mold in the shape of the animal's parts. The earth then turns to rock over time. If the mold gets filled in with other rock materials over time, the fossil is called a cast.

Long ago, this spider got trapped in sticky tree sap that hardened into amber.

Unlike the fossil remains of most dinosaur bones, the bones of this fossil saber-toothed tiger are actual bone.

Ancient Insects

Some small animals, or parts of animals, have been found in hardened tree sap called amber. Long ago, an insect might have become trapped in the sticky sap. Soon the sap would have completely covered the insect. Over a long period of time, the sap turned into a hard, yellow or reddish-brown substance called amber. Thin pieces of amber are usually clear enough to see through. What you see is the animal's actual body covering kept together for millions of years.

One other type of fossil is found in tar pits. Saber-toothed tigers and other extinct animals fell into these oily pools many thousands of years ago. The soft parts of their bodies broke down and left only the bones. These fossils are the actual bones of these animals.

1. ✓**Checkpoint** What are some ways that fossils form?

2. **Math** in Science If a modern-day lizard is 10 meters long and a dinosaur skeleton is 3 times as long, how long is the dinosaur skeleton?

How Animals Today Compare to Those of Long Ago

Fossils can tell us how animals have changed over time. Dinosaurs are extinct. An extinct animal is a kind of animal that no longer lives on Earth. As you can see from the pictures, some animals today look like animals of long ago.

Fossils also tell us how Earth has changed over time. The drawing on the next page shows what the Badlands of South Dakota probably looked like more than 65 million years ago. At that time, dinosaurs like *Tyrannosaurus rex* roamed the area. Plant fossils found in layers of rocks near *T. rex* fossils tell scientists that the climate was hot and wet when *T. rex* lived. Plants could grow year-round. That is why you see plants in the drawing of the *T. rex*.

T. rex's habitat has changed a great deal. The photo in the drawing shows what the Badlands look like today. Only animals that are adapted to hot, dry conditions can live there now.

Although this collared lizard is a tiny, modern-day reptile, it resembles dinosaurs of long ago.

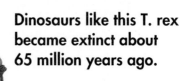

Dinosaurs like this T. rex became extinct about 65 million years ago.

56

Today the Badlands in South Dakota are almost like a desert.

This is one artist's view of how a *T. rex* might have looked. It also shows its habitat.

✓ Lesson Checkpoint

1. Describe four kinds of fossils.

2. What can fossils tell us about extinct animals?

3. **Writing in Science** **Expository** In your **science journal,** write about what might have happened to *T. Rex* when its environment changed.

Investigate What can you learn from an imprint?

Imprint fossils are one type of fossil. Scientists can learn about animals that lived long ago by studying the imprints they made.

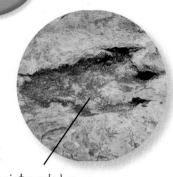

imprint made by a dinosaur

Materials

cup with prepared plaster of Paris

spoon

paper plate and paper towels

bowl of water

What to Do

1 Put plaster of Paris onto a plate.

Spread the plaster of Paris around with a spoon.

Be careful!

2 Wet one of your hands.

Do not put plaster of Paris into a sink. It can clog the drain.

3 Spread the fingers of your wet hand. Press the palm side of this hand into the plaster of Paris.

4 Remove your hand from the plaster. Let the imprint dry.

Wipe the plaster of Paris off your hand. Use paper towels. Wash your hands thoroughly.

5 Make a chart to record what you **observe** about your hand and its imprint.

Appearance	
Imprint	**Hand**

Explain Your Results

1. How is your imprint like your hand that made it? How is it different?

2. **Infer** How might an imprint fossil of an animal be like the animal that made it? How might it be different?

Go Further

Use a hand lens to observe and study tiny details. If you wish, make sketches or diagrams. Use your ruler to measure your hand and its imprint.

Comparing Speeds of Fish

There is a great difference in the swimming speeds of fish. Generally, larger fish can swim faster than smaller fish. The bar graph below shows the greatest swimming speeds of six different fish.

Greatest Swimming Speeds

Fish:
- Barracuda
- Southern Bluefin Tuna
- Marlin
- Salmon
- Sailfish
- Swordfish

Kilometers per hour: 0 5 10 15 20 25 30 35 40 45 50 55 60 65 70 75 80 85 90 95 100 105 110

1. Which of the six fish is the fastest swimmer?
   A. Salmon
   B. Marlin
   C. Barracuda
   D. Sailfish

2. Which of the six fish is the slowest swimmer?
   F. Swordfish
   G. Barracuda
   H. Southern Bluefin Tuna
   I. Marlin

3. Use the data in the graph to list the six fish in order from slowest to fastest.

Lab zone **Take-Home Activity**

Use an almanac, the Internet, or other sources to find the most recent Olympic records for swimming. Make a graph or a chart showing the record times for each swimming event.

Chapter 2 Review and Test Prep

Use Vocabulary

adaptation (page 48)	**migrate** (page 52)
hibernate (page 52)	**pupa** (page 45)
inherited (page 48)	**trait** (page 40)
larva (page 45)	**vertebrate** (page 40)

Use the vocabulary word from the list above that best completes each sentence.

1. An animal with a backbone is called a(n) _____.

2. In an early stage of life, when a butterfly eats and grows, it is called a(n) _____.

3. Some animals need much less food to survive when they _____.

4. Something that helps a living thing survive is called a(n) _____.

5. If something passes on from a parent to its offspring, it is _____.

6. The stage in the life cycle of a butterfly during which it changes into an adult is called the _____.

7. Sometimes animals move to another place, or _____, to find better food or shelter.

8. A feature passed on to an animal from its parents is a(n) _____.

Explain Concepts

9. Explain why different animals can be grouped in more than one way.

10. Why does inheriting an adaptation help offspring survive?

11. What is the difference between instinct and learned behavior?

12. Describe the changes a frog goes through during its life cycle.

Process Skills

13. **Infer** If a fossil skull has flat teeth, what do you think this animal probably ate?

14. **Predict** A hawk has feet with sharp claws on them to help it catch small animals to eat. What kind of feet would you predict a bird that swims would have?

Sequence

15. Use the signal words to put the stages of the life cycle of a frog in the correct sequence.

First

Next

Finally

Test Prep

Choose the letter that best completes the statement or answers the question.

16. Fossils tell us

(A) about animals that lived in the past.

(B) about how Earth has changed.

(C) how today's animals are similar to past life.

(D) all of the above.

17. The earliest stage in a frog's life cycle is a(n)

(F) pupa.

(G) egg.

(H) chrysalis.

(I) tadpole.

18. Which of the following is an animal without a backbone, or invertebrate?

(A) insect

(B) bird

(C) mammal

(D) amphibian

19. Explain why the answer you chose for Question 18 is best. For each of the answers you did not choose, give a reason why it is not the correct choice.

20. Writing in Science

Descriptive Suppose a hungry fox comes upon a porcupine. Write a paragraph describing what happens between the two animals.

Paul Sereno:
Expert Dinosaur Hunter

Paul Sereno

When he was a boy, Paul Sereno liked to go on nature hikes with his brothers. He brought home insects to add to his collection. Paul went to college to study art. However, while he was in college, Paul decided he wanted to become a paleontologist—a scientist who studies ancient life.

Paleontologists like Dr. Sereno try to find fossils to piece together the story of what life was like long ago. Dr. Sereno and his team have found many new kinds of dinosaurs.

Dr. Sereno's team made a discovery in Africa. A giant claw lying in the desert was the first clue. Dr. Sereno and his team carefully dug for more bones. They found a huge skeleton of a dinosaur. Its skull was long with crocodile-like teeth. Dr. Sereno named the new dinosaur *Suchomimus* which means "crocodile mimic."

It sometimes takes years for paleontologists to make sense of what they find. But their hard work often leads to new discoveries.

Lab zone Take-Home Activity

Using library resources and the Internet, research newly discovered dinosaurs. List them by name, type of dinosaur, and where found.

You Will Discover

- what an ecosystem is.
- different kinds of land ecosystems.
- different kinds of water ecosystems.

Chapter 3

Where Plants and Animals Live

How are ecosystems different from each other?

environment

ecosystem

desert

grassland

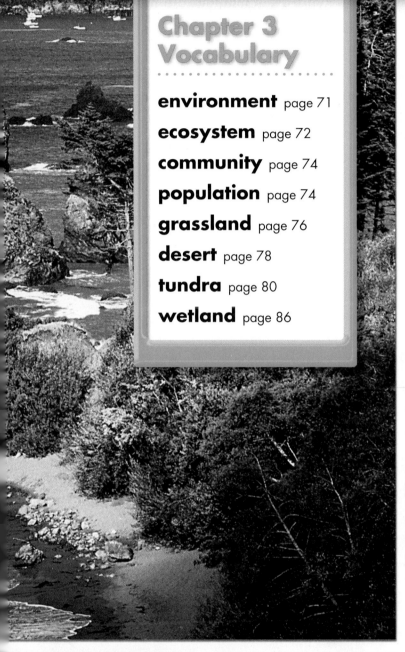

Chapter 3 Vocabulary

population

community

tundra

wetland

Explore In which soil do grass seeds grow best?

How will you know in which soil grass seeds *grow best*? Should *grow best* mean the most blades of grass grow, the tallest blades grow, or the greenest blades grow? You decide. **Make an operational definition** of *grow best*. Begin with the words "Grow best means. . . ." Then say what you will observe that will tell you which *grows best*.

Materials

3 paper cups and a pencil

sandy, clay, and loam soils

grass seeds and cup with water

spoon and masking tape

Process Skills

You explained how you would decide in which soil the seeds *grow best.* When you told what you would **observe** to make this decision, you **made an operational definition**.

What to Do

1. Make 4 holes in the bottom of each cup with a pencil. Half fill the cups with soil. Put 2 spoonfuls of water in each cup.

   Label the cups.

2. Sprinkle $\frac{1}{2}$ spoonful of grass seeds in each cup. Lightly cover the seeds with more soil. Set the cups in a warm place with bright light.

sandy soil

clay soil

loam soil

3. Add 1 spoonful of water to each cup daily for 2 weeks. **Observe** each cup daily.

Explain Your Results

What is your **operational definition** of *grow best*? In which soil did the seeds *grow best* according to your definition?

Main Idea and Details

A number of different things might all be connected to a **main idea**. These are called **details.** Learning to find the **main idea and details** helps you understand what you read. Look at the graphic organizer. The main idea is at the top. The details help support the main idea.

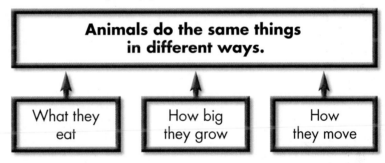

Science Article

Home Address

Animals live in different places. Some live in forests. Others live in lakes or oceans. Different animals have different body coverings. Some have fur or feathers. Others have scales. The animals' body coverings help them live where they do.

Apply It!

Make a graphic organizer like the one shown above. Use it to help you **make an operational definition** about what you read and what you have observed. Write the main idea at the top. Fill in the missing details that support the main idea from the science article.

You Are There!

You are standing where the ocean meets the land. You can feel the warm sunlight on your face. You hear the waves rush onto the shore. You wiggle your toes in the cool, damp sand. Birds circle above you. This is a terrific place for you to visit. What makes it a perfect place for certain plants and animals to live?

AudioText

What are ecosystems?

Plants and animals meet their needs in the place where they live. Living things depend on other living things and nonliving things around them.

Places for Living Things

Each living thing needs a certain environment. A living thing's **environment** is everything that surrounds it. An environment has living parts and nonliving parts. The living parts include plants, animals, and other living things. The nonliving parts include the Sun's rays, air, water, and soil.

The Sun's rays are necessary for life. They warm the air, water, and soil to the temperature that living things need. Sunlight helps plants make food.

Climate shapes each environment. Climate is the weather in a place all year. For example, one place might have cold, wet winters and hot, dry summers. Another place might be cold and dry all year long.

Water and soil are important parts of each environment. Water falls as rain and snow, and enters the soil. Soils differ in the way they hold this water. Each type of plant needs a certain amount of water and a certain kind of soil.

1. ✓**Checkpoint** Name four nonliving things that are part of a plant's or animal's environment.

2. **Art** in Science Draw a picture that shows the things that you need that your environment provides. Write labels on your drawing of what these things are.

Parts of an Ecosystem

In an environment, living and nonliving parts act on each other or interact. These interacting parts make up an **ecosystem.**

The living parts of an ecosystem depend on nonliving parts. For example, coastal redwood trees need sunlight, soil, and air. They also need a lot of water. There is plenty of rain in winter, but no rain falls in the summer. So, in the summer, the trees get water instead from fog that rolls in from the ocean.

The living parts of an ecosystem also depend on one another. For example, some sea birds scoop up fish from the ocean. Then they fly inland to nest in the redwood trees.

Special Homes

The place where a living thing makes its home is its habitat. A habitat has all the things that a plant or animal needs to live. For example, a habitat can be a branch of a redwood tree in which a bird builds a nest. The habitat gives plants light, air, water, living space, and pollinators. It gives animals food, water, shelter, and living space. If any of these things is missing, something will change. The habitat might no longer be able to support some plants or animals. These plants or animals may struggle to survive, die, or try to move to a new habitat.

Interacting Parts of an Ecosystem	
Living	**Nonliving**
plants	light/heat
animals	air/water
other living things	rocks/soil

The plants, animals, and environment of this coastal ecosystem interact with one another.

This coastal California redwood tree shares its environment with other plants and animals.

Dune grass has tough roots. They help the plant survive in strong wind, bright sunlight, and shifting sand.

1. ✓**Checkpoint** What is an ecosystem?

2. **Main Idea and Details** Read the caption about the dune grass. Give the main idea. List details that support it.

Groups Within Ecosystems

Coyotes roam the rough brush called chaparral on coastal hillsides in Southern California. All the living things of the same kind that live in the same place at the same time are a **population.** A group of coyotes make up a population.

Coyotes hunt California ground squirrels. The ground squirrels eat plants and live in burrows within openings in the chaparral. All the populations that live together in the same place make up a **community.** The coyotes, ground squirrels, and chaparral plants help make up a community. The populations in a community depend on each other.

A coyote hunts ground squirrels.

Ecosystems Change

Ecosystems change over time. The change starts when one part of the ecosystem changes. This change causes other parts of the ecosystem to change. For example, in one winter the chaparral might get more rain than usual. Plants grow more. Ground squirrels now have more food than usual. This may cause the population of ground squirrels to grow.

The rise in the number of ground squirrels affects the coyotes. The population of coyotes can grow because coyotes find plenty of food.

If a winter has less rain than usual, plants provide less food. Less food supports fewer ground squirrels. As a result, the population of coyotes remains small or decreases.

All the coyotes in one place make up a population.

74

Fires move quickly through chaparral. This provides space, water, and sunlight for new plants to grow.

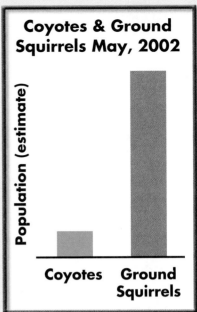

Coyotes & Ground Squirrels May, 2002

Population (estimate)

Coyotes | Ground Squirrels

More food than usual supports a large ground squirrel population.

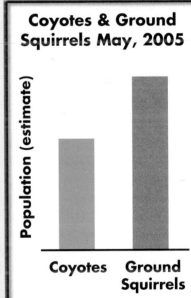

Coyotes & Ground Squirrels May, 2005

Population (estimate)

Coyotes | Ground Squirrels

If the ground squirrel population is large, the coyote population might become large too.

✓ Lesson Checkpoint

1. How do coyotes, ground squirrels, and plants interact in their environment?

2. What might happen to plants and animals if there is more rain than usual?

3. **Writing in Science** **Descriptive** Describe a population in your **science journal**. Then describe the community to which your population belongs.

Which ecosystems have few trees?

Different places on Earth have different climates. Some land ecosystems have climates that support only a few trees.

Grassland

Think about looking out over a wide, grassy field. A strong summer breeze makes the tops of the grasses move like waves on the ocean. A **grassland** is a kind of land ecosystem. It has many grasses and flowering plants, but few trees. A climate of cool or cold winters and hot summers supports grasslands. The climate includes little rain, so the soil is dry. Trees cannot grow well in this soil. They need more water. The trees grow mostly in the wetter soil along rivers and creeks.

Many grasses grow well in this kind of habitat. They survive because they have deep roots. These roots help the plants in many ways. When grazing animals, fire, or the cold winters kill the plants above ground, the roots survive. Deep roots also help the plants find water in the dry, hot summers.

Some grasslands get more rain than others. Tall-grass prairies grow in the wetter eastern parts of the Midwest. Short-grass prairies grow farther west where less rain falls.

Climate in the Kansas Grassland		
Average Temperature (°C)		Average Yearly Rainfall (cm)
Summer	Winter	
20	2	90

Map Fact
This is the Konza Prairie in Kansas. Like other parts of the Midwestern United States, it is grassland.

Winters are cool or cold in the grasslands. Deep roots help the plants store food for winter.

Many kinds of insects, such as this grasshopper, live in grasslands.

Once huge herds of bison roamed the grasslands. Now, only a few herds remain.

1. ✔️**Checkpoint** What is a grassland?

2. 🎯 **Main Idea and Details** Tell the main idea about grasslands. Give supporting details.

Desert—A Surprising Ecosystem

A **desert** is an ecosystem that gets very little rain. Days are often hot, but the nights are cool or even cold. Many people think of deserts as nothing but sand. However, most desert ecosystems are full of life. Desert plants and animals can live with little rainfall. Some plants, including cactuses, store water in their leaves or stems.

During the day, you might see a lizard warming itself on a rock. But many desert animals rest out of sight during the hottest time of day. Some stay in underground tunnels. Others find a shady spot under a plant. At night the desert comes alive. Animals come out of their hiding places to search for food.

Climate in a Desert		
Average Temperature (°C)		Average Yearly Rainfall (cm)
Summer	Winter	30
30	10	

Yucca plants provide shade and cover for small animals like snakes and lizards. Small birds eat the fruits.

This sidewinder rattlesnake usually hunts at night. It kills small animals for food.

This desert bobcat warms itself on a sunny rock in winter. At night, it hunts for birds and other small animals.

Map Fact

Joshua Tree National Park is a desert ecosystem in southern California. Joshua trees are a kind of yucca plant, which grows only about 6 centimeters a year. More than 78 kinds of birds nest in the park.

1. ✓ **Checkpoint** Why do certain plants do well in deserts?

2. **Writing** in Science **Expository**
Write a newspaper article about desert animals. Explain why they are active at night.

Tundra—Land of Long Winters

The **tundra** is a cold, dry, land ecosystem. It is in the very northern part of the world. Parts of Alaska are tundra. Winters there are long and cold. Snow falls and cold winds blow. Summers are short and cool. The snow melts in summer, but the soil below the surface does not become soft. It stays frozen all year.

Summer days are very long in the tundra. In some places, the summer Sun shines 24 hours a day. Winter days are very short. Some places get no sunlight at all in winter.

Many plants cannot grow in this climate. For example, few trees grow in the tundra. Their roots cannot grow in frozen soil. Small plants grow here instead. These include grasses and wildflowers.

In summer, the melting snow forms ponds in the tundra. Many ducks, geese, and swans nest near these ponds. Other birds also nest in the tundra. In summer, there are millions of insects for them to eat. Most tundra birds travel to warmer places during winter.

Climate in the Tundra		
Average Temperature (°C)		Average Yearly Rainfall (cm)
Summer	Winter	
6	30° below 0	10

Caribou travel in large herds. In winter, they find food by digging through the snow with their front hooves.

What type of plant is missing in this tundra? Trees! Their roots cannot grow into the frozen soil. Grasses and wild flowers grow close to the ground.

Lichens grow in clumps close to the ground. It is the main winter food of caribou.

Wolves usually travel in groups, or packs, to hunt for food. They hunt caribou, hares, and lemmings. Other large hunters include brown bears and golden eagles.

✓ Lesson Checkpoint

1. What is the coldest land ecosystem?

2. List three kinds of land ecosystems.

3. **Math** in Science A day is 24 hours long. Nome, Alaska, has about 21 hours of daylight on July 4. How many hours of darkness does it have? Nome has 4 hours of daylight on January 1. How many hours of darkness does it have then?

What are some forest ecosystems?

There are ecosystems that have different kinds of thick forests. Each kind of forest ecosystem has its own plants and animals.

Coniferous and Deciduous Forests

Coniferous forests grow mainly in northern North America, Europe, and Asia. They grow in places that have cold, snowy winters. They grow where summers are warm and dry. These forests have many conifers such as spruce, fir, and pine. The tree leaves look like needles.

Few plants grow under coniferous trees. Mosses are a common type of plant that grows there. Lichens also grow under the conifers. Still, many animals live in coniferous forests. They can find food and shelter.

Climates where deciduous forests grow are generally warmer than those of coniferous forests. Deciduous forests get rain in summer and snow in winter. Deciduous forests can have oak, maple, and beech trees. They drop their leaves in the fall. For part of the year, sunlight reaches the forest floor. Many shrubs and other plants can grow there. These plants provide habitats for animals.

1. ✔**Checkpoint** How are coniferous and deciduous forests alike and different?

2. **Writing** in Science **Descriptive** Write a short story about walking through an evergreen forest or a deciduous forest. Describe what you see, hear, and feel.

Climate in a Coniferous Forest		
Average Temperature (°C)		Average Yearly Rainfall (cm)
Summer	Winter	
8	−20	50

North American Coniferous Forest

Moose eat twigs, bark, roots, and young stems of woody plants. In summer, they feed on water plants like water lilies.

Climate in a Deciduous Forest		
Average Temperature (°C)		Average Yearly Rainfall (cm)
Summer	Winter	
25	5	160

Many insects and birds live in deciduous forests. Woodpeckers eat beetles that dig into tree trunks.

North American Deciduous Forest

Beavers use their sharp teeth to cut forest trees and branches. They build dams of sticks and mud across streams.

83

Tropical Forests

Where could you find a spider so big that it eats birds? These spiders live in a tropical forest. These forests grow near the equator. Tropical forests can have a climate that is warm and rainy all year long. The many tall trees let little sunlight reach the forest floor. Some of the trees can be 35 meters tall—taller than a ten-story office building. Plants such as orchids grow on the trees.

Most animals of the tropical forest live in the trees. Some spend their whole lives there.

Some of these animals, such as bats, can be found in many different tropical forests. Others live in only certain forests and not in others. For example, many kinds of beetles live in only one forest in Brazil. They are found nowhere else. The tropical rainforest has huge numbers of insects. No one has ever named them all.

Woolly monkeys live in South America. They live in trees and eat fruits, leaves, seeds, and some insects.

Rainbow lorikeets live in the tropical forests of eastern Asia and Australia. These noisy birds eat nectar, flowers, seeds, and fruit.

Climate in a Rainforest		
Average Temperature (°C)		Average Yearly Rainfall (cm)
Summer	Winter	
25	25	300

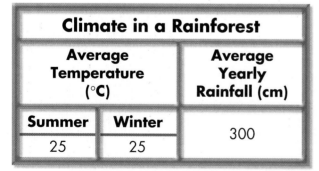

These red stinkbugs live in tropical forests.

Venomous snakes, such as this palm viper, live in tropical forests. Most snakes eat frogs, lizards, and other small animals.

✓ Lesson Checkpoint

1. What kind of climate can tropical forests have?

2. List three kinds of forests.

3. **Writing** in Science **Descriptive** Write a paragraph in your **science journal** describing how climate affects different kinds of forests.

What are water ecosystems?

Water ecosystems can have fresh water, salt water, or both.

Freshwater Ecosystems

Freshwater ecosystems include lakes, ponds, rivers, and streams. Lakes and ponds are water surrounded by land. Rivers and streams are moving water. Rain or melting snow supplies water for most lakes and rivers. Springs that flow from underground supply water for others. Many plants and animals live in lakes and rivers.

The Everglades in south Florida is a large wetland. A **wetland** is low land that is covered by water at least part of the year. Water flows very slowly through the Everglades south to Florida Bay. This "river of grass" is very wide. But its water is very shallow. Trees, grasses, and water plants live there. Animals such as fish, bears, and birds live there, too.

Florida Everglades

Many large Florida springs are the winter homes of manatees. These slow-moving mammals eat water plants.

Map Fact

There are hundreds of springs that empty into lakes and rivers in Florida. Weeki Wachee Spring in central Florida supplies the water for the Weeki Wachee River, shown here.

1. ✓**Checkpoint** Name four kinds of freshwater ecosystems.

2. **Technology** in Science Use the Internet to find out about the plants and animals that live in the Everglades. Make a list of these plants and animals.

Saltwater Ecosystems

Oceans cover much of Earth's surface. Ocean water contains salt. The ocean is shallow along the shore. Clams, crabs, kelp, fish, and coral live here. Otters, seals, and sea birds swim and dive for fish.

The open ocean gets very deep, but most life is in the top 200 meters of water. Very small animals feed on tiny algae that make food. Large fish and whales also live here. The deep ocean is dark and cold, and it has little food. Few animals live here.

Many rivers flow into the ocean. Fresh water from the river can mix with salt water from the ocean. Salt marshes can form in these areas. Salt marshes are wetlands that contain special plants and animals. These living things are able to live in salty water and soil. Many plants grow in salt marshes. These wetlands also contain a muddy soup of tiny living animals. Some are too small to see with just your eye. Many kinds of fishes, crabs, and other ocean animals begin their lives in salt marshes.

Life in the Oceans	
Kinds of Living Things	275,000 kinds
Longest Animal	Blue Whale, 33 meters
Longest Fish	Whale Shark, 12 meters
Fastest Ocean Animal	Sailfish, 30 meters per second

This reef cuttlefish can squirt a jet of water out of its body. This helps it escape from an enemy.

Map Fact

The Great Barrier Reef is a huge coral reef. It is along the eastern coast of Australia. Australia is in the southern Pacific Ocean.

Australian Great Barrier Reef

A coral is an animal about the size of an ant. It builds a hard, rocky skeleton around itself for protection. Millions of corals build a coral reef.

✓ **Lesson Checkpoint**

1. Where do most corals live?

2. Where is most life found in the oceans?

3. **Writing in Science** **Narrative** Find out about an animal that lives in salty water. Then write a story in your **science journal** about that animal. Title your story (Name of your animal)—This Is Your Life!

Investigate How can you show that mold needs food?

You have learned that animals of each ecosystem find the food they need where they live. In this activity you will show that in order to stay alive and grow, mold must get the food it needs. If it is in an "ecosystem" without the food it needs, it will not grow.

Materials

gloves

moldy strawberry

hand lens

bread slice
(without preservatives)

foil square

2 plastic bags

dropper

cup with water

Process Skills

You **interpret data** when you use data from an investigation to answer a question.

What to Do

1 **Observe** the mold on the strawberry. Draw what the mold looks like.

Be careful!

Wear gloves.

2 Lightly rub some mold off the strawberry onto the bread. Do the same for the foil.

3 Put the bread in a bag. Put the foil in another bag. Use a dropper to add 10 drops of water to the 2 spots where the mold was rubbed.

4 Seal the bags. Put them in a warm, dark place.

After you seal the bags, do not reopen them.

5 After 4 days, observe the bags. Draw pictures of any mold growing in the bags.

Mold gets the energy needed for growth from the bread.

Drawings of Observations		
Mold on Strawberry	**Mold on Bread**	**Mold on Foil**

Explain Your Results

1. In which bag did mold grow?

2. **Interpret Data** Which has the food that mold needs to grow, the bread or the foil? Explain.

Go Further

Does mold need light to grow? Investigate. Use a camera to keep a record.

Math in Science

Comparing Data

The major grasslands of North America are located in six areas, as shown on the map. The tall-grass prairie, the mixed-grass prairie, and the short-grass prairie together are known as the Central Prairies.

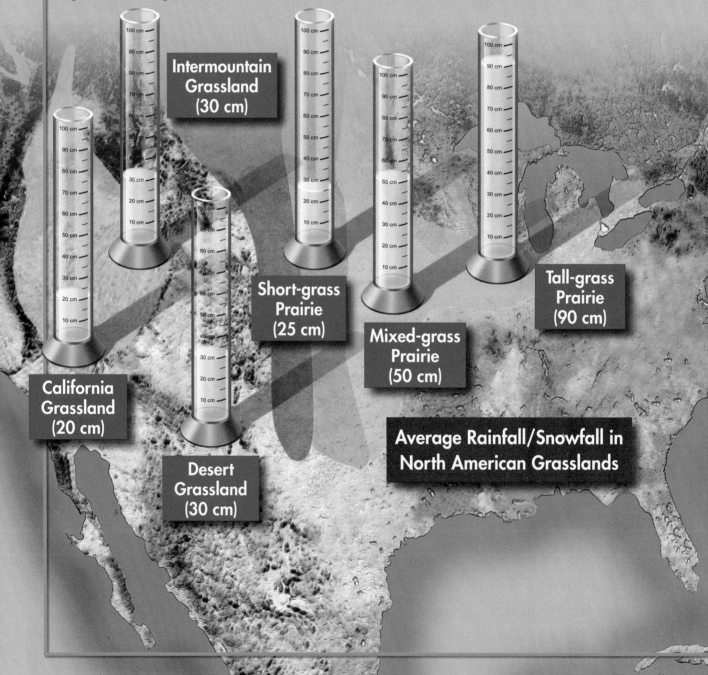

Intermountain Grassland (30 cm)

California Grassland (20 cm)

Desert Grassland (30 cm)

Short-grass Prairie (25 cm)

Mixed-grass Prairie (50 cm)

Tall-grass Prairie (90 cm)

Average Rainfall/Snowfall in North American Grasslands

eTools Take It to the Net
sfsuccessnet.com

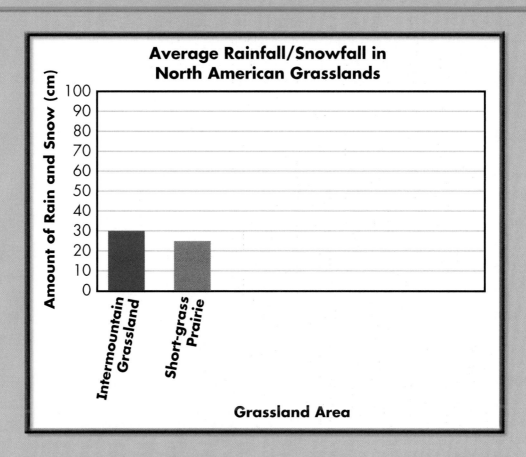

Average Rainfall/Snowfall in North American Grasslands

Amount of Rain and Snow (cm)

100 90 80 70 60 50 40 30 20 10 0

Intermountain Grassland

Short-grass Prairie

Grassland Area

Use the map and the graph to answer each question.

1 Copy the bar graph on grid paper and complete it. Your graph should show the data for all six grasslands.

2 Which describes how the amount of rain and snow in the Central Prairies changes?

A. increases from west to east   B. decreases from west to east

C. increases from north to south   D. decreases from north to south

3 Which grassland gets the most rain and snow? Which gets the least?

Lab zone Take-Home Activity

Use the library or the Internet to find data about rainfall and snowfall amounts in any type of ecosystem in North America. Show the data on a bar graph.

Chapter 3 Review and Test Prep

Use Vocabulary

community (page 74)	**grassland** (page 76)
desert (page 78)	**population** (page 74)
ecosystem (page 72)	**tundra** (page 80)
environment (page 71)	**wetland** (page 86)

Use the term from the list above that best completes each sentence.

1. Low land that is often covered by water is a(n) _____.

2. All the moose that live in one place are a(n) _____.

3. Everything that surrounds a living thing is its _____.

4. An ecosystem with hot days and little rain is a(n) _____.

5. All the populations living in the same place form a(n) _____.

6. The ecosystem that is coldest and farthest north is the _____.

7. All the living and nonliving things that interact in an area form a(n) _____.

8. An ecosystem with many grasses and few trees is a(n) _____.

Explain Concepts

9. Explain how dry soil and frozen soil affect the types of plants that grow in them. Give examples.

10. Explain how chaparral, coyotes, and ground squirrels depend on each other.

11. Explain how some desert plants are able to have enough water.

Process Skills

12. Wheat and oats are cereal grasses. **Infer** in which ecosystem these farm crops would grow best.

13. Desert snakes eat kangaroo rats. **Predict** what would happen to the population of rats if the population of snakes grew larger.

14. **Interpret data** Use the data table below. Find the difference between the greatest yearly rainfall and the least.

Forest	Yearly rainfall
Coniferous forest (Alaska)	70 cm
Deciduous forest (Maryland)	120 cm
Tropical forest (Hawaii)	1,234 cm

 Main Idea and Details

15. Draw the graphic organizer below. Choose an ecosystem for the main idea. Fill in details that support the main idea.

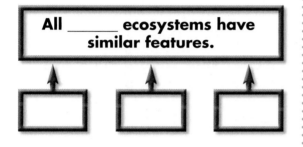

All _____ ecosystems have similar features.

 Test Prep

Choose the letter that best completes the statement or answers the question.

16. A group of trout that live in a river make up a(n)
- (A) community.
- (B) population.
- (C) habitat.
- (D) ecosystem.

17. Which ecosystem has a warm, rainy climate?
- (F) tropical forest
- (G) tundra
- (H) evergreen forest
- (I) desert

18. Which populations might live in a wetland?
- (A) corals, whales, and fish
- (B) coniferous trees, foxes, and woodpeckers
- (C) birds, alligators, and grasses
- (D) cactuses, rattlesnakes, and bobcats

19. Explain why the answer you selected for Question 16 is best. For each of the answers you did not select, give a reason why it is not the best choice.

20. **Writing** in Science
Expository Write a paragraph about a plant or animal and how it survives in a desert ecosystem.

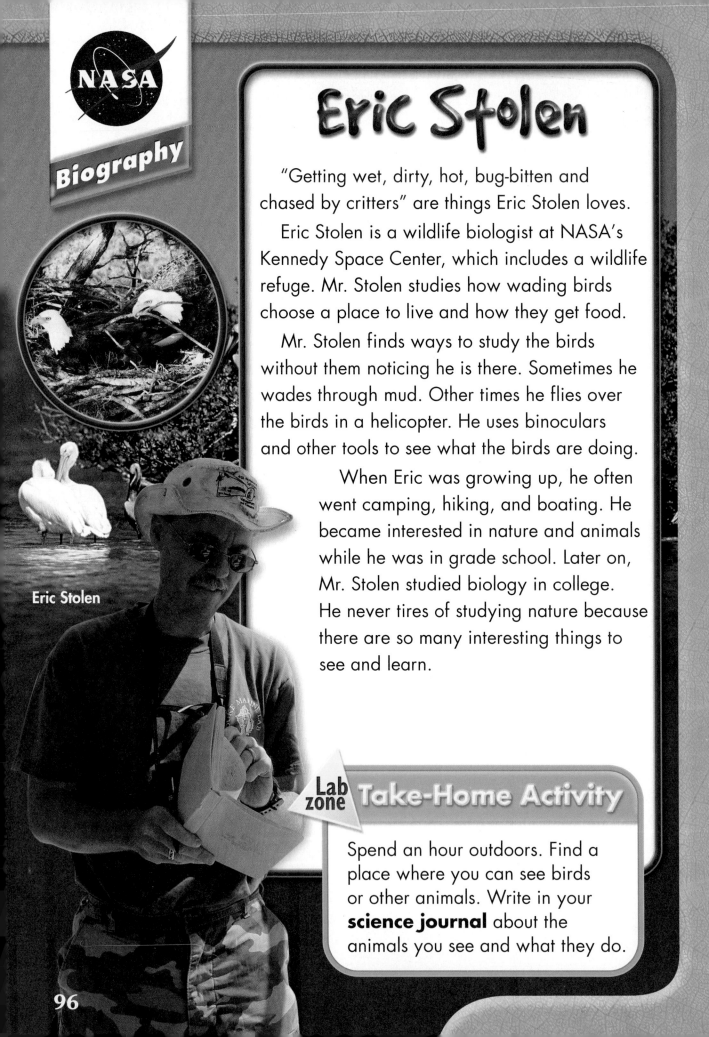

Biography

Eric Stolen

"Getting wet, dirty, hot, bug-bitten and chased by critters" are things Eric Stolen loves.

Eric Stolen is a wildlife biologist at NASA's Kennedy Space Center, which includes a wildlife refuge. Mr. Stolen studies how wading birds choose a place to live and how they get food.

Mr. Stolen finds ways to study the birds without them noticing he is there. Sometimes he wades through mud. Other times he flies over the birds in a helicopter. He uses binoculars and other tools to see what the birds are doing.

When Eric was growing up, he often went camping, hiking, and boating. He became interested in nature and animals while he was in grade school. Later on, Mr. Stolen studied biology in college. He never tires of studying nature because there are so many interesting things to see and learn.

Eric Stolen

Lab zone Take-Home Activity

Spend an hour outdoors. Find a place where you can see birds or other animals. Write in your **science journal** about the animals you see and what they do.

Chapter 4

Plants and Animals Living Together

You Will Discover

- ways that plants and animals interact.
- how food energy moves through an ecosystem.
- what a healthy environment for people includes.

online
Student Edition
sfsuccessnet.com

How do plants and animals interact?

consumer

producer

herbivore

98

Chapter 4 Vocabulary

decomposer

decay

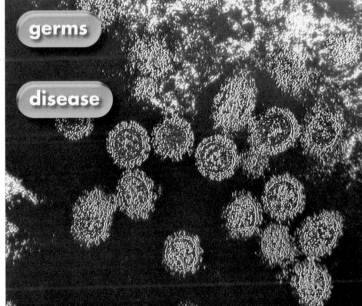

germs

disease

omnivore

carnivore   predator

competition   prey

Explore How do pill bugs stay safe?

Materials

plastic jar

soil, dead leaves, lettuce

cup with water

spoon

4 pill bugs

cheesecloth

rubber band

Process Skills

When you **infer** why pill bugs might roll into a ball, you use what you have **observed** about pill bugs and what you already know about safety.

What to Do

1 Make a habitat for pill bugs.

2 Use the spoon to gently put pill bugs into the habitat. Add 3 spoonfuls of water. Cover the jar.

Notice how a pill bug can roll into a ball. In a ball, its hard body covering helps protect its soft belly. A pill bug also may hide in dark places to avoid enemies.

cheesecloth
rubber band
lettuce
dead leaves
layer of soil

3 **Observe** the pill bugs for 5 minutes each day for one week. Describe what they do.

Explain Your Results

1. **Infer** How might rolling into a ball help a pill bug stay safe?

2. Why might pill bugs need lettuce or other plants in their habitat?

How to Read Science

Draw Conclusions

A good reader can put together facts and then build a new idea, or a conclusion. The conclusion should make sense and be supported by the facts. You might use a graphic organizer to show a conclusion.

Science Article

What's on the Menu

Shrews need food to be active. They find a lot of pill bugs to eat under rotting logs. One type of spider eats only such bugs. Toads, lizards, and birds eat pill bugs, too.

Apply It!

Make a graphic organizer like the one shown. Fill it in with three facts from the paragraph above. Then **infer** a conclusion. Show how the facts led to the conclusion.

Facts   **Conclusion**

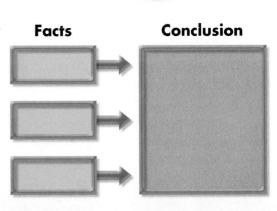

You Are There!

You are floating in clear ocean water. You look down through a face mask. You see a school of small fish. They swim left, right, up, and down. They all move together. Suddenly the school turns. You blink with surprise. When you look again, the school is gone! Where did the fish go? Why were they swimming together like that?

AudioText

How do living things interact?

Living things may affect each other when they interact. The interactions can be helpful, harmful, or neither.

Ways Living Things Interact

Living things interact in different ways. Their interactions may help them survive. Study the examples in the chart. Those living in groups help each other. One kind of living thing might help another kind without being helped in return. Or different kinds might help each other.

Ways Living Things Interact		
Helping in Groups	Members of a herd protect each other.	
One Kind Helping Another	A tree helps a flower get light.	
Two Kinds Helping Each Other	While it drinks flower nectar, an insect spreads pollen among the flowers.	

1. ✓**Checkpoint** List three ways in which living things might interact.

2. **Writing in Science** **Narrative** In your **science journal** describe a day during which you helped as a member of a group. Describe how the group helped you.

One bee may find flowers. Then it will fly back to the beehive and move in a certain way. This "dance" tells the other bees where the flowers are.

A grown barnacle is about 5 cm wide. It grabs food from the water that the whale swims through.

Living in Groups

Animals that live together might all help protect the group from predators. Together, the animals may be safer than each animal alone. For example, prairie dogs live in groups. Coyotes and golden eagles eat them. Coyotes hunt on the ground. Eagles hunt from the sky. Prairie dogs take turns standing watch at their burrow openings. If any prairie dog senses danger, it whistles. At this sound, the whole group runs and hides. All the prairie dogs stay hidden until the danger has passed.

One Kind of Living Thing Helping Another Kind

Notice the barnacles on the whale. Some barnacles swim through the ocean and attach to the skin of a whale. A barnacle usually spends its whole life attached to the same whale.

The barnacle opens and closes its shell to catch food as the whale moves through the water. The barnacles do not harm the whales. They don't help the whales either. In this partnership, only one partner is helped— the barnacle.

Helping One Another

Some kinds of living things help each other. The moth seen here shares its life with only one kind of yucca plant.

The moth helps the yucca by carrying pollen from another yucca. The yucca helps the moth by giving it a habitat and food for its young. The moth lays her eggs in the flower pods. Each larva hatches in the pods and eats some of the seeds the flower pod makes.

The cleaner fish is another example. Several kinds of small fish clean larger fish. They eat pests off the big fish. The cleaner fish gets a meal. The other fish gets clean and stays healthy.

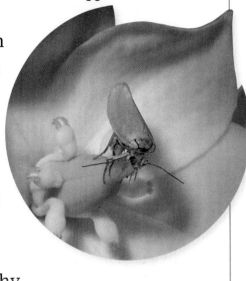

A yucca moth provides a ball of sticky pollen from another yucca. In exchange it lays its eggs in the flower.

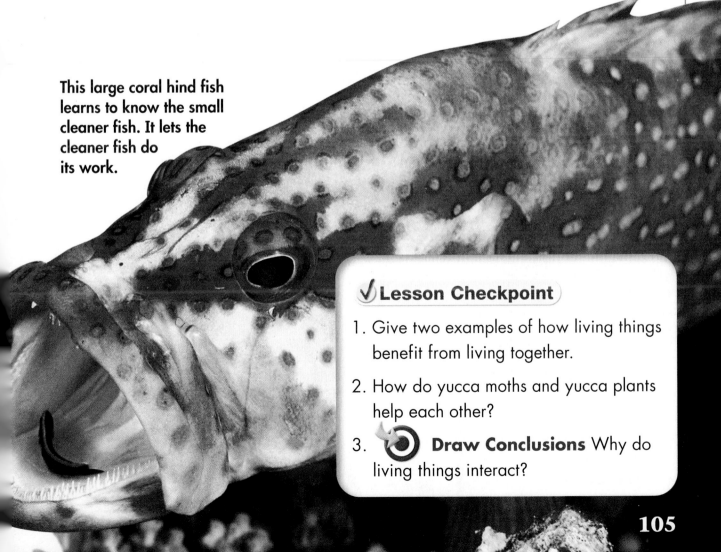

This large coral hind fish learns to know the small cleaner fish. It lets the cleaner fish do its work.

✔ Lesson Checkpoint

1. Give two examples of how living things benefit from living together.

2. How do yucca moths and yucca plants help each other?

3. **Draw Conclusions** Why do living things interact?

How do living things get energy?

Plants get energy from the sun. Animals get energy from plants or from other animals that eat plants.

Sources of Energy

Green plants make their own food. A living thing that makes its own food is a **producer.** Producers use energy from sunlight to make food out of matter from the air and soil.

Many living things cannot make their own food. They must get their energy from food that they eat. A living thing that eats food is a **consumer.**

Kinds of Consumers

Some consumers eat plants, others eat animals, and some eat both. A consumer that eats only plants is an **herbivore.** A consumer that eats only animals is a **carnivore.** A consumer that eats both plants and animals is an **omnivore.**

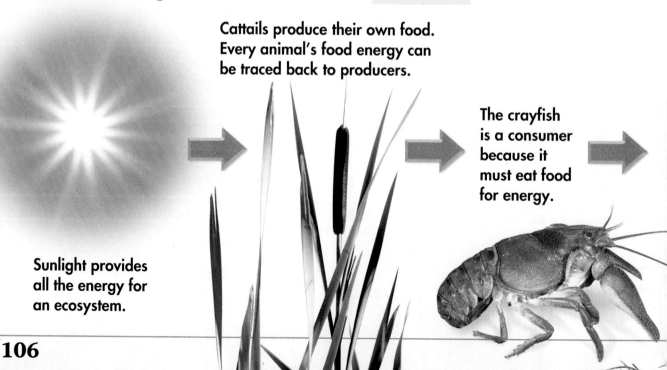

Cattails produce their own food. Every animal's food energy can be traced back to producers.

The crayfish is a consumer because it must eat food for energy.

Sunlight provides all the energy for an ecosystem.

Sheep are herbivores. They eat only plants.

A wolf is a carnivore. It eats only meat.

A bear is an omnivore. It eats both plants and animals.

Food Chains

Energy passes to living things within food chains. Food chains are groups of producers and consumers that interact in a special way. A consumer eats a producer. The producer passes energy to that consumer. That consumer may then become **prey** for another consumer. Prey is any animal that is hunted by others for food.

The prey passes energy on to a **predator.** A predator is a consumer that hunts for food. In this way, energy can move from a producer to a predator. As each living thing uses food energy, some energy is given off as heat.

The raccoon is an omnivore. It eats crayfish, other animals, and plants.

✓ Checkpoint

1. Trace the transfer of energy through a food chain that includes raccoons, crayfish, cattails, and sunlight.

2. **Art** in Science Draw a food chain that shows how grass, a cow, and a person drinking milk are connected.

107

Energy in a Food Web

A food chain is simple. Energy moves from one type of living thing to another. Real life is not so simple. Energy often moves in many different ways. It might transfer from one kind of producer to many kinds of consumers. One kind of consumer might be prey for more than one kind of predator.

Energy flow in a community forms a web. A food web is made up of more than one food chain. Food webs tie a community together. Each part of a web affects other parts.

An example of a food web is found on the Great Plains. Prairie grasses grow there. They are producers. Energy flows from the grasses to the animals that eat them. These animals include prairie dogs and mice. Prairie dogs are prey for ferrets and golden eagles. Ferrets are prey for badgers. So energy can flow through the food web from grasses to golden eagles and badgers.

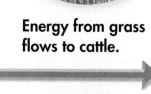

Energy from grass flows to cattle.

Energy from grass flows to prairie dogs.

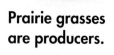

Prairie grasses are producers.

Energy from grass flows to mice.

A Changing Food Web

If one part of a food web is removed, other parts change. For example, prairie dogs once built large colonies on the grassy plains. Then cattle began to feed on these same plains. This reduced the habitat for prairie dogs. Many prairie dogs also became sick and died. As a result, the number of prairie dogs was reduced.

Removing one part of the food web caused a number of things to happen. The cattle had more food, but ferrets had less. With fewer prairie dogs to eat, ferrets no longer had the food they needed. Ferrets began to die out.

This, in turn, affected predators of ferrets, such as badgers. Now badgers had to look for other food. Golden eagles and foxes also hunt prairie dogs. They too had to get more food energy from other kinds of prey, such as mice. All this can happen when one part of a food web is removed.

Ferrets eat mostly prairie dogs. Energy flows to the ferrets.

Badgers eat ferrets. Energy flows to the badgers.

Golden eagles eat prairie dogs and mice. Energy from these animals flows to the eagles.

✔ Lesson Checkpoint

1. How did reducing the number of prairie dogs affect ferrets?

2. How does the loss of prairie dogs affect eagles and foxes?

3. **Draw Conclusions** Tell what happens when a food chain is broken.

The young trees in this forest compete for sunlight and room to grow.

This male bower bird competes with other males to attract females to its nest.

Many different animals compete for water in dry places.

How do living things compete?

Maybe you have tried to fit under an umbrella with another person to stay dry. You had to compete with the person for shelter. Living things often compete with one another. Usually they compete for food, water, and room to live.

Competing for Resources

Picture yourself in a dark, cool forest. The treetops form a roof high above you. Few small trees are growing. Why? They struggle to get enough energy from sunlight to grow. The small trees are in **competition** with one another. When two or more living things need the same resources, they are in competition. Since the tall trees in this forest get most of the sunlight, the small trees compete for the light that is left.

Living things compete for many kinds of resources besides light. These resources include food, water, and living space. The winners in these competitions survive. The losers might not survive.

SciLinks Take It to the Net sfsuccessnet.com | keyword: competition code: g3p110

Predators and Prey

Many predators may compete for the same prey. Faster, stronger ones might catch more food. For example, some hunting birds may get more food by stealing prey caught by the other birds. Predators with greater ability are more likely to survive and reproduce. They pass these valuable traits on to their young.

Different types of predators may compete with each other. Lions and hyenas might want the same prey, for example. The lions hunt and kill the prey. Then the hyenas fight the lions and try to steal it.

Animals that are prey also compete. Deer that are stronger or healthier than others are more likely to protect themselves. They are better able to escape from predators.

The lions have killed the prey. But the hyenas are not afraid to compete for as much of this food as they can get.

√ Checkpoint

1. What do living things compete for?

2. **Writing in Science** **Expository** Write a short paragraph in your **science journal** explaining why living things compete.

Purple loosestrife competes with other plants for space.

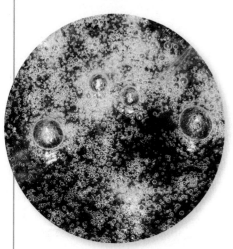

Sea gulls compete with humans for living space.

Too much algae can lead to too little oxygen that fish and tadpoles need.

Other Kinds of Competition

Some living things compete for space. Purple loosestrife is a plant that competes in this way. Years ago, someone brought this plant to the United States. It grew well near rivers. Animals here do not eat loosestrife, so it grew and spread. Now purple loosestrife takes space away from other plants. It is winning the competition for space in many places.

Sometimes animals and humans compete for space. People move to places where animals live. Then they see coyotes in their backyards or sea gulls nesting on their beaches.

Living things may compete for oxygen. Algae are like plants. They provide oxygen and food for fish and other living things. If too many algae grow, some will block the light needed by the others. These other algae die. Many tiny consumers of dead algae grow and use up the oxygen in the water. Fish and frogs must then compete for the oxygen that is left.

A Competition Cycle

Competition can follow a cycle. For example, lemmings are small mammals that live in the tundra. If there is plenty of grass for them to eat, the population grows quickly. Soon, less food is available because so many lemmings are eating it. After three years, too many lemmings are competing for too little food. Many lemmings leave to find food elsewhere. The population of lemmings is reduced. Then the grass can grow back. The cycle begins again.

Competition between these lemmings for food can follow a cycle over time.

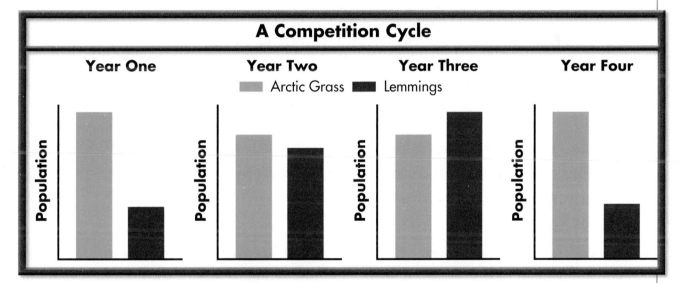

A Competition Cycle

Year One	Year Two	Year Three	Year Four

Arctic Grass   Lemmings

Year One	Year Two	Year Three	Year Four
There is plenty of arctic grass for lemmings to eat.	The population of lemmings grows. The amount of grass goes down.	The population of lemmings grows. There is not enough food. Many lemmings leave or die.	With fewer lemmings, the grass grows back. Once again there is enough food.

✓ Lesson Checkpoint

1. Why do living things compete with one another?

2. What kind of living thing usually survives in a competition?

3. **Draw Conclusions** Explain the pattern of change in the lemming population over time.

113

How do environments change?

Plants and animals can change their environment. Natural events, such as fire, can change the environment too. These changes affect plants and animals that live in the environment. Changes often occur in patterns.

Living Things Cause Change

People often change the environment to better suit their needs, but they are not the only ones. For example, when a beaver builds a dam, many changes occur. Water backs up behind the dam. Then a new wetland habitat grows. Fish, birds, and many other types of animals can now live there.

The dams, however, flood places that were once dry. What do you think happens to the living things that once lived on dry land? Some look for new homes. They might compete for space in nearby places. Others may not survive.

Beavers change the environment when they build their homes and dams of sticks and mud.

This place was once a grassy meadow. How has this beaver dam changed it?

Natural Events Cause Change

Natural events also change environments. For example, hurricanes can change coastlines. They wash away beaches and knock down trees. They can cause terrible floods.

Floods change environments too. They kill plants and wash away birds' nests. Floods spread thick blankets of mud. They also carry rich soil from one place to other places.

Too little water also causes changes. Little rain falls during a drought. Plants die from lack of water. If animals cannot find enough water, then they may die or move to other places.

The Mississippi River sometimes floods. The floodwater carries rich soil down the river. When floodwater drains off the land, it leaves behind a layer of soil.

High winds and water will change this environment.

Few plants, animals, or humans can live in a drought area.

✓ Checkpoint

1. Describe ways that living things and natural events can cause an environment to change.

2. **Writing** in Science **Descriptive**
Write a paragraph or a poem in your **science journal** about one change you have seen in your environment.

Living Things Return

On May 18, 1980, the volcano Mt. St. Helens erupted in the State of Washington. This eruption was huge. Winds carried clouds of ash around the world.

The blast changed the local environment. It knocked over trees. It burned whole forests. Rivers of mud covered large areas.

There were few signs of life after the eruption. Over time, however, wind carried the seeds of grasses, flowers, and trees to the mountain. New plants began to grow. Soon spiders and beetles arrived. Birds returned to live in the standing dead trees. Each new change allowed more kinds of plants and the animals that depend on them to live there again. Today, even elk live on Mt. St. Helens. The mountain is filled with life once more.

In September 2004, Mt. St. Helens rumbled to life again. An active volcano can bring sudden change at any time.

Mt. St. Helens erupts.

Fires also change environments. Fires happen often in forests and grasslands. Lightning may strike a tree. A burning branch falls to the ground. Then a fire creeps along the forest floor. It removes small plants competing for space to grow. However, the plants that do not burn will have more living space. Also, ash from fires is good for the soil. It helps plants to grow.

Eruptions and fires are examples of events that cause change. The changes often kill plants and destroy animal homes. The changes, however, may improve habitats for other plants and animals.

✓ **Checkpoint**

1. Explain how fire is a change that can improve growing conditions for plants.

2. **Art** in Science   Draw a forest before a fire. Then draw the forest on fire. Finally, draw the forest five years later.

Very few plants remained after the volcano erupted.

New life has returned to the mountain.

Ground fires kill plants but help new plants grow.

This young pine grows fast in an area cleaned by fire.

This burnt stump gives a spruce seedling a place to grow.

117

Many years will go by before these Douglas fir seedlings become full-grown trees.

Smaller trees compete for sunlight because they are shaded by tall trees.

Map Fact

Forests of tall coniferous trees grow in the temperate rain forest along the coast of the State of Washington.

Patterns of Change

Living things change together. These changes often happen in patterns. Let's look at one growth pattern. It takes place in a cool, misty forest in the northwestern United States. Douglas firs and western hemlocks are two kinds of trees that live there. Their life cycles are connected.

Douglas fir trees have cones which are often knocked off by squirrels. Seeds from the cones sprout on the forest floor where they compete for sunlight and other resources. A few survive and grow into giant trees. Some of these giants grow old, die, and fall.

Mushrooms and other decomposers feed on the dead trees. A **decomposer** is a living thing that breaks down waste and living things that have died. This action is called **decay.** Decay returns certain materials to the soil. The trees had taken these materials from the soil in order to grow. Decomposers cause the dead tree to slowly crumble into the soil.

Western hemlock trees live in the same forest. Seeds from their cones land on the decaying Douglas fir logs. The decaying nurse logs supply things that help young seedlings to grow. Also, light reaches logs in the open where the giant trees once stood. The hemlock seeds sprout and grow quickly.

SciLinks Take It to the Net
sfsuccessnet.com
keyword: decomposer
code: g3p118

In time, the hemlocks become tall trees. They provide homes for squirrels, spotted owls, and many other animals. When the trees come to the end of their lives, carpenter ants and other organisms go to work. They build nests in the decaying tree trunks. After some years, these trunks fall to the ground. Soon they decay and become part of the soil.

This example shows the life cycle of two trees. Their life cycles are connected. In fact, the life cycles of many living things are connected.

These mushrooms are decomposers. They find this dead log a good food source.

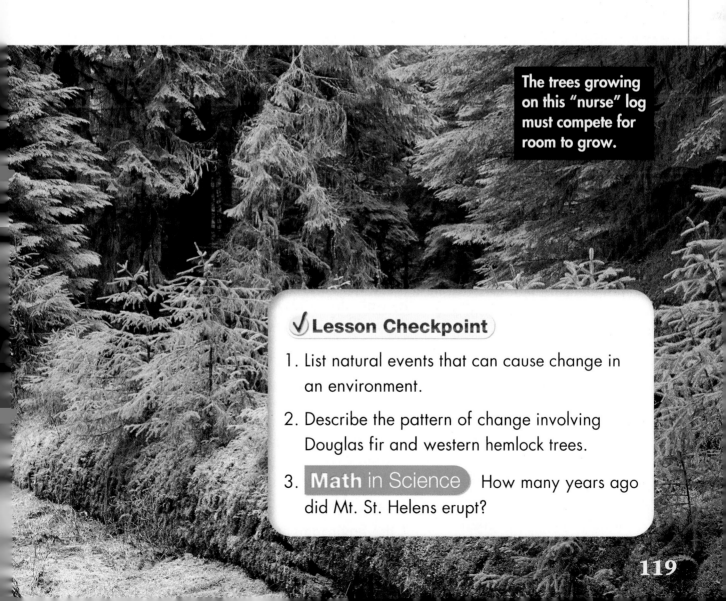

The trees growing on this "nurse" log must compete for room to grow.

✓ Lesson Checkpoint

1. List natural events that can cause change in an environment.

2. Describe the pattern of change involving Douglas fir and western hemlock trees.

3. **Math** in Science How many years ago did Mt. St. Helens erupt?

119

What is a healthy environment for people?

People find what they need for life in their environment. The environment affects how people live.

What People Need

Like all living things, people need food to live. Most people buy food at a store. That food comes from farms and ranches. Some people have the job of making sure the food we eat is safe.

People need water that is safe to drink and air that is safe to breathe. People also need shelter to protect them from the weather. Shelter helps keep people at a comfortable temperature.

People need a clean environment. Wastes must be removed. Garbage may be taken to places such as landfills.

The water from this fountain was purified, or made clean, at a water treatment plant.

✔ Checkpoint

1. Name three things people need to survive.

2. **Writing** in Science **Persuasive**
   Write a paragraph in your **science journal** explaining why we should protect the environment.

Basic Needs of People

Food

The food you eat may come from close by. It may be grown thousands of miles away. Fresh food is shipped on airplanes, boats, and trucks. Other foods may be canned or frozen before being shipped.

Water

In some countries, people get their water from streams. In the United States, most water comes from wells or from special lakes. These special lakes are called reservoirs.

Shelter

Shelter changes according to where someone lives. In hot places, people need cool living spaces. In cold places, they need warm ones. In cities, people often live in large buildings.

Air

Fewer people live outside the cities. In these open spaces there are fewer cars and factories. As a result, the air is often cleaner.

Clean Environment

Everyone should help protect the environment. The environment affects the health of the people living in it.

Healthful Foods

To be sure you are getting all the vitamins, minerals, and other nutrients your body needs, you must eat a variety of healthful foods. This variety includes whole grains, fruits, and vegetables, as well as nuts, fish, eggs, dairy foods, and meats. Your body also needs a good amount of water each day.

To be kept healthful, food should be stored carefully. Fresh fruits and vegetables should be washed and kept in a cool place. Fish, eggs, dairy foods, and meats must be wrapped and kept cold. Using food while it is still fresh is also important.

Cooks and others who handle food must have clean hands and clean tools. Their tools include knives and cutting boards as well as mixers, bowls, spoons, and forks.

Drinking juice is a healthful choice.

Dairy products help bones grow strong.

Vegetables such as carrots and broccoli make good snacks.

Eat fruit, such as grapes, every day.

Fish contain materials your body needs to grow.

From Food to Energy

What happens to food after you eat it? The body's digestive system goes to work. It breaks foods down into a form that our bodies can use to live and grow. These are the main parts of the digestive system.

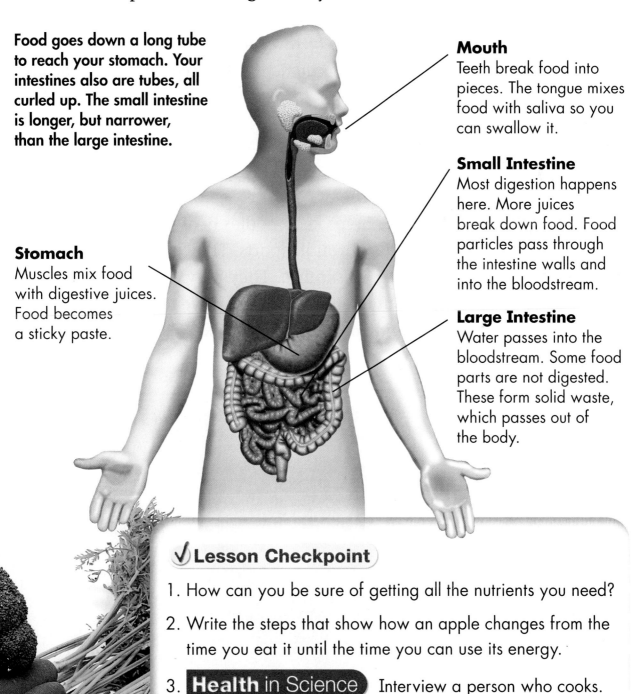

Food goes down a long tube to reach your stomach. Your intestines also are tubes, all curled up. The small intestine is longer, but narrower, than the large intestine.

Stomach
Muscles mix food with digestive juices. Food becomes a sticky paste.

Mouth
Teeth break food into pieces. The tongue mixes food with saliva so you can swallow it.

Small Intestine
Most digestion happens here. More juices break down food. Food particles pass through the intestine walls and into the bloodstream.

Large Intestine
Water passes into the bloodstream. Some food parts are not digested. These form solid waste, which passes out of the body.

✓ Lesson Checkpoint

1. How can you be sure of getting all the nutrients you need?

2. Write the steps that show how an apple changes from the time you eat it until the time you can use its energy.

3. **Health in Science** Interview a person who cooks. Find out how that person chooses and takes care of food.

123

How can people stay healthy?

People want to be as healthy as possible. There are many things they can do to help keep their bodies healthy.

Exercise

Safe, regular exercise is important. People in good shape have the energy to work, play, and feel good about themselves.

Exercise helps keep bodies healthy. Some people get exercise through sports. They go biking, swimming, or skating. They play basketball or soccer. But exercise does not have to be a sport. House and yardwork can be exercise too.

When you rest, your heart beats about ninety times per minute. It beats faster when you exercise.

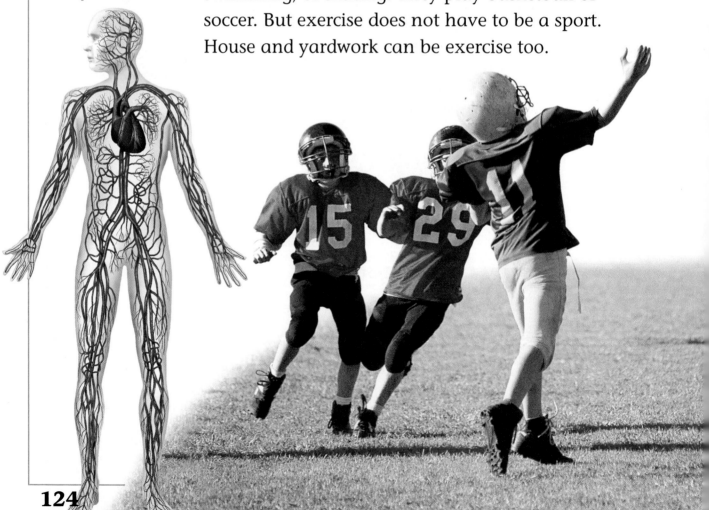

Exercise keeps a person's lungs, heart, and muscles strong. These are parts of your body systems. For example, your lungs are part of your respiratory system. They put oxygen from the air you breathe into your blood. Your heart and blood vessels are part of your circulatory system. The heart pumps blood through blood vessels. Blood carries oxygen and other materials to your muscles. Blood also carries wastes away from your muscles. Exercise helps your systems work together well so you stay in good shape.

People who feel good about themselves take care of their bodies. They eat a variety of good foods. They get enough exercise and rest. They avoid things that are unhealthy.

When you breathe in, air goes down a long tube called the windpipe. The windpipe divides into two tubes. Each tube leads to a spongy lung.

The proper equipment keeps these young football players safe.

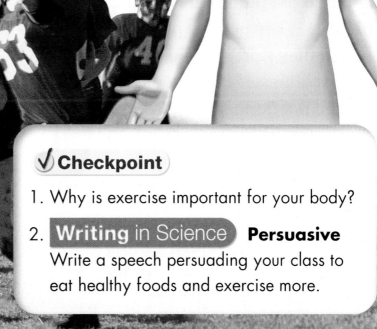

✓ **Checkpoint**

1. Why is exercise important for your body?

2. **Writing** in Science **Persuasive**
   Write a speech persuading your class to eat healthy foods and exercise more.

Avoiding Germs

Lin is sneezing. Shauna is coughing. Aidan has a runny nose and teary eyes. Several of their classmates are at home, sick with the flu. What are causing these illnesses? Germs.

Germs are very small living things or particles. Examples include bacteria and viruses. Many germs can make people ill. The pictures show germs that can cause disease. A **disease** is a condition in which the body or a part of the body does not work properly. You may have had one or more diseases such as the flu, chicken pox, or strep throat.

There are many other diseases that you have probably not had. These include measles, mumps, and whooping cough. Years ago, many people caught these illnesses. They were very dangerous. Today, children are protected from these diseases. They get this protection before they start school.

Most illnesses that people get are not dangerous. Still, no one likes to be sick. Everyone can help to stop the spread of germs.

This picture shows the virus that causes the flu. This picture was taken through a special, very powerful microscope.

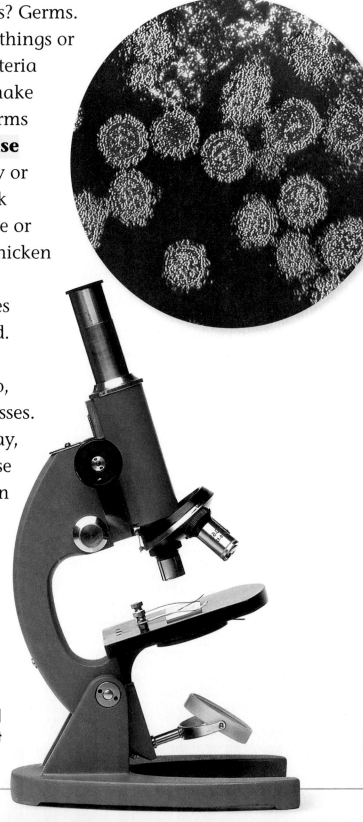

Microscopes are used to observe things that are very small.

The germs shown below cause whooping cough.

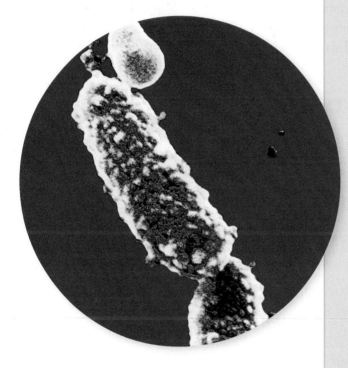

The germs that cause strep throat look like tiny beads.

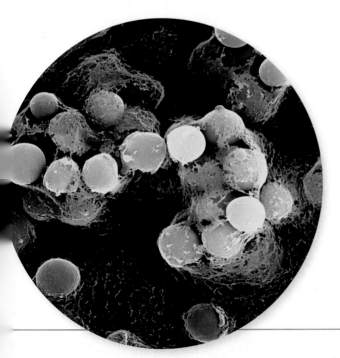

Stopping the Spread of Germs

People can help stop the spread of germs by remembering some simple rules.

- Stay home from school and work when you are ill.
- Wash your hands often, especially after using the restroom and before and after working with food.
- Cover your nose and mouth when you sneeze or cough. Wash your hands if you sneeze or cough into them.
- Clean and cover cuts and scrapes.

Wash your hands often with soap and warm water so that you don't spread germs.

✓ Lesson Checkpoint

1. How do your respiratory and circulatory systems work together?

2. Make a list of things you can do to stop the spread of germs.

3. **Technology** in Science
   Choose an illness to research. Find out its causes and possible cure. Use the Internet or other technology to help in your research.

127

Guided Inquiry

Investigate What can happen in a place without predators?

Without predators, a population of prey can starve. In this activity, your teacher will pick some students to be deer. All live in a place without predators. The deer pretend to eat the same kind of food (unpopped popcorn).

Materials

unpopped popcorn

What to Do

1 If you are picked to be a deer, line up on the side of the marked area. This is where you find food.

2 **Round A** When told, cross the area one deer at a time. Collect 5 pieces of food (unpopped popcorn) to "stay alive." Do not take more than 5 pieces.

Round	Number of Deer Alive at End of Round
Round A	
Round B	
Round C	
Round D	
Round E	

The number of rounds will depend on the number of deer and the amount of food supplied.

Record how many deer are alive at the end of each round. After each round your teacher will add food.

3 If you survive, you reproduce. Pick another student to join for the next round.

4 **Round B** Cross again and collect 5 more pieces of food.

Process Skills

You can use the **data** you **collect** during an investigation to help make an **inference**.

Deer line up here.

area where deer find food

5 Repeat until "starvation" begins. Make a bar graph to show the **data** you **collected**.

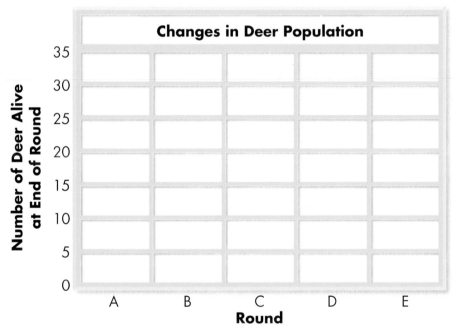

Changes in Deer Population

Number of Deer Alive at End of Round

35
30
25
20
15
10
5
0

A   B   C   D   E

Round

Explain Your Results

1. While there was plenty of food, how did the number of deer change? What finally happened?

2. **Infer** What can happen in a place without predators?

Go Further

What might happen if predators were added? Make a plan to answer this or a question of your own.

Math in Science

Health
By the Numbers

You have learned how important it is to choose the right foods for good health. It is also important to know how many Calories you need and how many are in the foods you eat.

Smiley Flakes
Serving Size 1 cup (30 grams)
Calories: 110
Total Fat: 2 grams
Cholesterol: 0 grams
Sodium: 210 milligrams
Carbohydrates: 23 grams
Fiber: 1 gram
Sugar: 1 gram

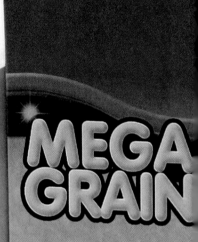

Mega Grain
Serving Size 1 cup (30 grams)
Calories: 165
Total Fat: 1 gram
Cholesterol: 0 grams
Sodium: 0 milligrams
Carbohydrates: 39 grams
Fiber: 3 grams
Sugar: 0 grams

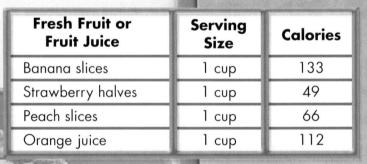

Fresh Fruit or Fruit Juice	Serving Size	Calories
Banana slices	1 cup	133
Strawberry halves	1 cup	49
Peach slices	1 cup	66
Orange juice	1 cup	112

Milk Products	Serving Size	Calories
Whole milk	1 cup	146
Reduced-fat milk (2%)	1 cup	122
Low-fat milk (1%)	1 cup	102
Fat-free milk (Skim)	1 cup	83

Tools Take It to the Net
sfsuccessnet.com

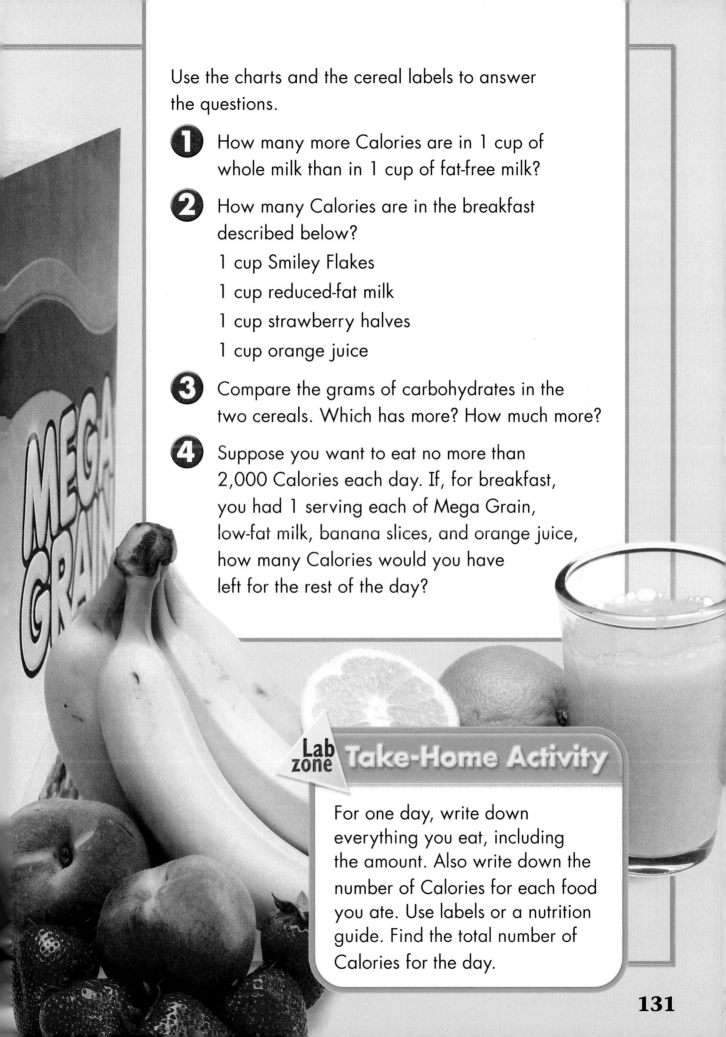

Use the charts and the cereal labels to answer the questions.

1 How many more Calories are in 1 cup of whole milk than in 1 cup of fat-free milk?

2 How many Calories are in the breakfast described below?
1 cup Smiley Flakes
1 cup reduced-fat milk
1 cup strawberry halves
1 cup orange juice

3 Compare the grams of carbohydrates in the two cereals. Which has more? How much more?

4 Suppose you want to eat no more than 2,000 Calories each day. If, for breakfast, you had 1 serving each of Mega Grain, low-fat milk, banana slices, and orange juice, how many Calories would you have left for the rest of the day?

Lab zone Take-Home Activity

For one day, write down everything you eat, including the amount. Also write down the number of Calories for each food you ate. Use labels or a nutrition guide. Find the total number of Calories for the day.

Chapter 4 Review and Test Prep

Use Vocabulary

carnivore (page 106)	**germs** (page 126)
competition (page 110)	**herbivore** (page 106)
consumer (page 106)	**omnivore** (page 106)
decomposer (page 118)	**predator** (page 107)
decay (page 118)	**prey** (page 107)
disease (page 126)	**producer** (page 106)

Write the vocabulary word or words from the list above that best completes each sentence.

1. A(n) _____ eats only animals while a(n) _____ eats only plants.

2. Bacteria and viruses are _____, which can cause _____.

3. A(n) _____ is a consumer that hunts another for food.

4. A(n) _____ is a living thing that must eat food to get energy,

5. A(n) _____ makes its own food.

6. _____ happens between living things that have a need for the same resources.

7. A(n) _____ eats both plants and animals.

8. _____ happens when a(n) _____ breaks down a living thing that has died.

9. _____ is an animal that is hunted by others.

Explain Concepts

10. Trace the flow of energy from beginning to end in the following food chain: a ferret eats prairie dogs which eat grasses and other plants.

11. Explain why some plants that are put into a new area can become dangerous weeds.

12. Explain the helpful and harmful effects ground fires have on plants in a forest community.

13. Describe ways to stay healthy.

Process Skills

14. **Classify** the following living things as producers or consumers: prairie dog, whale, purple loosestrife, barnacle, Douglas fir.

15. Predict The lemming population keeps growing. There are just enough resources. Predict what might happen to the lemmings if their population grows more.

16. Interpret Data You collect data in a field next to a stream. You trap and count 16 field mice and 10 rabbits. A beaver dam floods the field. You trap and count 7 field mice and 4 rabbits. Interpret this data.

 **Draw Conclusions**

17. Make a graphic organizer like this one. Fill it in with three facts about whales and whale barnacles from the chapter. Then write a conclusion based on those facts.

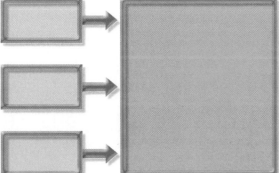

Facts   Conclusion

 Test Prep

Choose the letter that best answers the question.

18. Which living thing helps the second living thing in the pair to survive?
  Ⓐ barnacle–crayfish
  Ⓑ yucca moth–whale
  Ⓒ Douglas fir tree–western hemlock tree
  Ⓓ raccoon–cattail

19. Which of the following is true?
  Ⓐ Your lungs are a part of your circulatory system.
  Ⓑ Exercise maintains health.
  Ⓒ Washing your hands after coughing into them spreads germs.
  Ⓓ Nutrients pass through the walls of the intestine into the stomach.

20. Writing in Science
  Expository Write a short paragraph describing how yucca moths and the yucca plant interact.

Moon Trees

Astronaut Stuart Roosa took seeds with him into space.

Did you know there might be Moon trees growing where you live? You may be asking yourself, "What do Moon trees look like? Did they come from the Moon? Where are they growing on Earth?"

Well, Moon trees did not come from the Moon. They are trees grown from seeds that traveled to the Moon and back on the Apollo 14 mission in 1971.

Astronaut Stuart Roosa took the seeds into space. Astronaut Roosa worked for the U.S. Forest Service fighting forest fires before he joined NASA. He loved forests and wanted to protect them. He took seeds of pine, sycamore, redwood, Douglas fir, and sweet gum into space to honor the U.S. Forest Service.

A third-grade class in Indiana made this sign for their Moon tree. Astronaut Roosa's son, Col. Christopher Roosa, visited the tree with the students and their teacher.

MOON TREE

THIS SYCAMORE WAS GROWN FROM A
SEED THAT TRAVELED TO THE
MOON AND BACK ON
APOLLO XIV JANUARY 1971.
PRESENTED TO CAMP KOCH IN 1976
REDEDICATED APRIL 10, 2003

"LONG MAY OUR MOON TREE LIVE"

When the seeds were brought back to Earth, scientists examined them to see if space travel had changed them in any way. Then they were planted. No one knew what the trees would look like or even if they would grow.

The Moon trees grew until they were big enough to plant outside. People all over the world began to learn about the Moon trees. They wanted one of their own. In 1975 and 1976, the little trees were sent to places around the world. Most Moon trees were sent to schools, parks, and public buildings.

Today you can find a Moon tree growing near the Liberty Bell in Philadelphia. Another grows at the White House. Let NASA know if you find that a Moon tree is growing where you live.

You can see this Moon tree at the NASA Goddard Space Flight Center in Maryland.

Lab zone Take-Home Activity

Space travel might have had what effect on the Moon tree seeds and the way they would grow? Write a paragraph.

Park Ranger

Do you like being outdoors? Would you like to work outside with plants and animals? If so, then this career might be for you.

If you visit a national park, you will probably see park rangers. Park rangers have many tasks. They help visitors decide what to see and do during a visit. They plan programs, give talks, and lead hikes. They know about the plants, animals, and history of the park.

Park rangers also help take care of visitors. Rangers keep these visitors safe. They show them where to go in the park. They help visitors who are lost or hurt. They make sure that park rules are followed.

Sometimes fires start in parks. These might be caused by visitors or by lightning. Rangers help put out fires.

Most park rangers go to college. They may start working as rangers during the summer. They later take full-time jobs.

Lab zone Take-Home Activity

Locate the National Park Service site nearest to where you live. Find out and describe what the rangers there do.

Unit A Test Talk

Find Important Words

Finding important words and their meanings in a passage can help you answer test questions.

You can underline the important words as you read the passage. Some important words are underlined in the passage below.

All animals grow and change as they go through their life cycle. The first stage of an animal's life cycle is an egg. In mammals, eggs grow and develop inside the mother and the young are born. In other kinds of animals, such as birds and insects, the mother lays eggs outside of her body. The young develop in the eggs and then they hatch.

Some animals that hatch look like their parents. Baby chicks look like chickens. When a butterfly egg hatches, it is a caterpillar or <u>larva</u>. Larvae don't look like their parents. The larva develops and becomes a <u>pupa</u>. The pupa spins a covering over itself. Inside the covering, the pupa grows into a butterfly, just like its parent.

Use What You Know

To help you answer the questions, find the important words in the passage. As you read each question, decide which word choice is being described.

1. What is the first stage of an animal's life cycle?
- Ⓐ pupa
- Ⓑ larva
- Ⓒ adult
- Ⓓ egg

2. In which kind of animal do eggs grow and develop inside the mother until the young are born?
- Ⓕ insects
- Ⓖ mammals
- Ⓗ birds
- Ⓘ fish

3. What is the stage of a butterfly between a caterpillar and an adult?
- Ⓐ larva
- Ⓑ pupa
- Ⓒ egg
- Ⓓ seed

137

Unit A Wrap-Up

Chapter 1

How do the different parts of a plant help it live and grow?

- Most plants have roots, stems, leaves, and flowers. Each kind of part helps the plant grow, make food, or make seeds.
- Some kinds of plants have flowers. Other kinds have cones.

Chapter 2

How do different animals live, grow, and change?

- All animals begin as eggs. The eggs of some animals develop inside the mother while other animals lay eggs that hatch outside the mother.
- Some young animals look like their parents. Other young animals must go through different stages of development before they look like their parents.

Chapter 3

How are ecosystems different from each other?

- Environmental conditions determine the major types of ecosystems.
- Grasslands, deserts, tundras, and forests are land ecosystems. Water ecosystems include fresh water, salt water, or both.

Chapter 4

How do plants and animals interact?

- Animals interact by living in groups and sharing jobs. Some animals benefit by living with other kinds of animals. Animals often compete for the things they need to survive.

- Plants and animals belong to food chains. In a food chain plants produce their own food, some animals eat the plants for food, and other animals get food by eating animals.

Performance Assessment
Group Materials for Making Food

Plant leaves make food for the plant. The cards show the materials that are used to make food and the materials that are made. Place all the materials that a leaf uses to make food to the left of the leaf card. Place all the materials that the leaf makes to the right of the leaf card. What do plant leaves use to make food? What do plant leaves make?

leaf

oxygen

carbon dioxide

energy from the Sun

water

sugar

Read More About Life Science!

Look for books like these in the library.

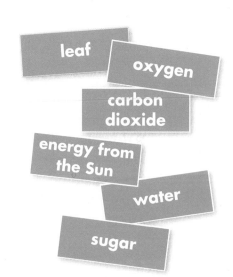

Nature's Green Umbrella
Tropical Rain Forests   Gail Gibbons

How Do BIRDS Find Their Way?
by Roma Gans • illustrated by Paul Mirocha

SMART ABOUT
George Washington Carver
THE PEANUT WIZARD

Full Inquiry

Experiment How can a garden spider move across its web?

A garden spider weaves a web with some threads that are sticky. Prey stick to these threads. Other threads are not sticky. The spider can walk on both types and not get stuck. In this **experiment**, you make a model to find out how a garden spider reaches its prey without getting stuck in its own web.

Materials

Spider Web Pattern

regular tape

double-stick tape

eraser

toothbrush

Process Skills

Every experiment must have a **hypothesis**, a testable statement.

Ask a question.

A garden spider has stiff hairs on the ends of its legs. Do these hairs help the spider move across its web?

State a hypothesis.

If a spider has stiff hairs on its legs, then will getting stuck in its web be more likely or less likely than if it did not have these hairs, or do these hairs have no effect? Write your **hypothesis**. You will use a **model** to help test your hypothesis.

Identify and control variables.

In the model used in this experiment, the **variable** that you change is the structure of a spider's "leg" (hairs or no hairs). The variable you **observe** is whether or not the "spider" gets stuck. The structure of the "web" is a variable you keep the same.

Test your hypothesis.

1 Make a model of $\frac{1}{4}$ of the web of a garden spider. Use the Spider Web Pattern.

2 First put down double-stick tape where shown. The double-stick tape is a model of the sticky threads of a spider's web.

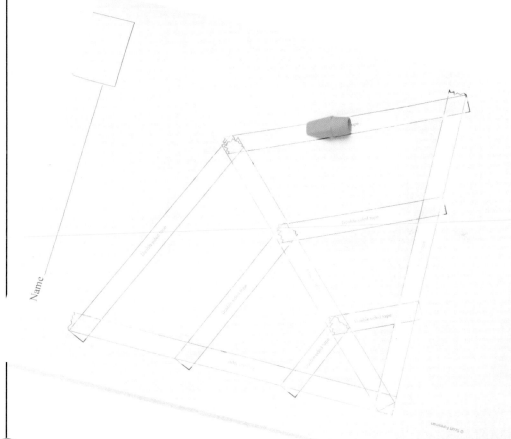

3 Next put down regular tape. The regular tape is a model of the non-sticky threads of a spider's web.

4 Put an eraser on one of the sticky outer pieces of tape. The eraser is a model of a spider's prey.

5 Start your "spider" at the center point of the web. Tap the side of the toothbrush without the brush along one of the non-sticky pieces of tape. Move from the center toward the prey. Record what happens.

6 When you reach the outer ring, tap across the sticky tape. Record what happens.

The eraser is the spider's "prey."

The toothbrush acts like a spider's leg. The side with the brush is a model of the spider's leg with stiff hairs. The side without the brush is a model of what a spider's leg would be like if the leg did not have stiff hairs.

7 Repeat steps 4 and 5, but this time use the side of the toothbrush with the brush.

Collect and record your data.

Model	Observations	
	Moving Across Non-Sticky "Thread" (regular tape)	**Moving Across Sticky "Thread"** (double-stick tape)
Without stiff hairs (side of toothbrush without brush)		
With stiff hairs (side of toothbrush with brush)		

Think of a way to use a diagram or a sketch of your model to show your observations. If your teacher wishes, explain your results orally or in writing.

Interpret your data.

What on the leg of a garden spider helps it easily reach its prey? How do you know?

State your conclusion.

Explain why a garden spider does not get stuck in its web. Compare your hypothesis with your results. **Communicate** your conclusion.

Tell how a model can help you make and test predictions. What did you learn from the model in this experiment?

Go Further

Butterfly wings are powdery. How does the powder help a butterfly escape from the sticky threads in a spider web? Design and carry out a plan for an experiment to answer this or other questions you have.

143

Science Fair Projects

Using Scientific Methods

1. Ask a question.
2. State a hypothesis.
3. Identify/control variables.
4. Test your hypothesis.
5. Collect and record your data.
6. Interpret your data.
7. State your conclusion.
8. Go further.

Germinating Seeds

Seeds need the right conditions to germinate and grow.

Idea: Use plastic cups, potting soil, and bean seeds to find out how well seeds germinate and grow with different amounts of water.

Growing Mealworms

When mealworm eggs hatch, they look nothing like their parents.

Idea: Use mealworms and a habitat to observe and record the different stages in their life cycle.

Selecting a Habitat

Different plants and animals need different habitats to survive.

Idea: Select a plant or an animal and make a habitat in which it can survive.

A Food Chain Model

Living things are connected by their need for food.

Idea: Choose a food chain and use paper chains with names or pictures to show the connections among the living things.

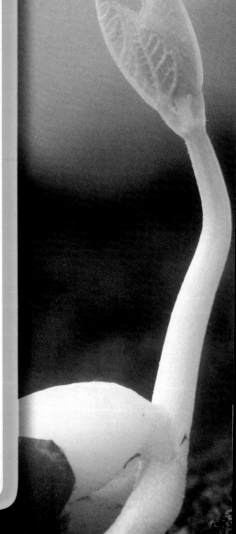

Metric and Customary Measurement

The metric system is the measurement system most commonly used in science. Metric units are sometimes called SI units. SI stands for International System because these units are used around the world.

These prefixes are used in the metric system:

  kilo- means *thousand*
  1 kilometer equals 1,000 meters
  centi- means *hundredths*
  100 centimeters equals 1 meter
  milli- means one-*thousandth*
  1,000 millimeters equals 1 meter

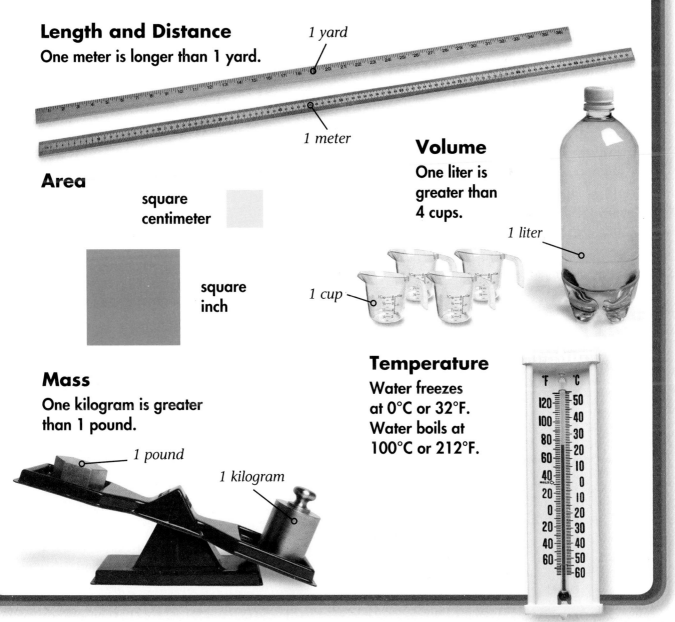

Length and Distance
One meter is longer than 1 yard.

1 yard

1 meter

Area

square centimeter

square inch

Volume
One liter is greater than 4 cups.

1 liter

1 cup

Mass
One kilogram is greater than 1 pound.

1 pound

1 kilogram

Temperature
Water freezes at 0°C or 32°F. Water boils at 100°C or 212°F.

Glossary

The glossary uses letters and signs to show how words are pronounced. The mark ′ is placed after a syllable with a primary or heavy accent. The mark ′ is placed after a syllable with a secondary or lighter accent.

To hear these words pronounced, listen to the AudioText CD.

A

absorb (ab sôrb′) to take in (p. 373)

adaptation (ad′ ap tā′ shən) trait that helps a living thing survive in its environment (p. 48)

asteroid (as′tə roid′) a small chunk of rock that orbits around the Sun (p. 457)

atmosphere (at′mə sfir) the blanket of air and gases that surround the Earth (p. 176)

atom (at′əm) one of the tiny particles that make up all of matter (p. 282)

axis (ak′sis) an imaginary line around which Earth spins (p. 424)

B

blizzard (bliz′ərd) a winter storm with very low temperatures, strong winds, heavy snowfall, and blowing snow (p. 183)

buoyancy (boi′ən sē) force exerted on an object that is immersed in a gas or liquid that tends to make it float (p. 286)

C

carnivore (kär′nə vôr) living things that hunt other animals for food (p. 106)

cause (kȯz) why something happens (p. 277, 311)

change of state (chānj uv stāt) physical change that takes place when matter changes from one state to another (p. 304)

chemical change (kem′ə kəl chānj) a change that causes one kind of matter to become a different kind of matter (p. 311)

classifying (klas′ə fī′ing) to arrange or sort objects, events, or living things according to their properties (p. 244)

collecting data (kə lek′ ting dā′ tə) to gather observations and measurements into graphs, tables or charts (p. 26)

communicating (kə myü′ nə kāt′ ing) using words, pictures, charts, graphs, and diagrams to share information (p. 324)

community (kəm myü′ nə tē) all the populations that live together in the same place (p. 74)

compare (kəm pâr′) to show how things are alike (p. 5, 245, 389, 453)

competition (kom′ pə tish′ən) struggle that happens when two or more living things need the same resource (p. 110)

EM2

compression wave (kəm presh′ən wāv) wave that has spaces where particles are squeezed together and spaces where particles are spread apart (p. 396)

computer (kəm pyü′ tər) tool which stores, processes, and gets electronic information (p. 485)

conclusion (kən klü′ zhən) decision reached after considering facts and details (p. 101)

condensation (kon′ den sā′ shən) the changing of a gas into a liquid (p. 157)

coniferous tree (kō nif′ər əs trē) does not lose its needle-like leaves in the fall (p. 16)

conservation (kon′ sər vā′ shən) the saving and wise use of natural resources (p. 250)

constellation (kon′ stə lā′ shən) a group of stars that make a pattern or shape (p. 438)

consumer (kən sü′ mər) living things that eat food (p. 106)

contrast (kən trast′) to show how things are different (p. 5, 245, 389, 453)

core (kôr) the innermost layer of Earth (p. 223)

crust (krust) the outermost layer of Earth (p. 223)

decay (di kā′) to break down, or rot (p. 118, 206)

deciduous (di sij′ü əs) loses its leaves in the fall and grows new ones in the spring (p. 14)

decomposer (dē′kəm pō′zər) a living thing that breaks down waste and things that have died (p. 118)

density (den′sə tē) measure of the amount of matter in a certain amount of space (p. 286)

desert (dez′ərt) an ecosystem that gets less than 25 cm of rainfall a year (p. 78)

details (di tālz′) individual pieces of information that support a main idea (p. 69, 357)

disease (də zēz′) the name we give an illness (p. 126)

earthquake (ėrth′kwāk′) a shaking of Earth's crust caused by sudden, shifting movements in the crust (p. 228)

ecosystem (ē′kō sis′təm) all the living and nonliving things that interact with each other in a given area (p. 72)

effect (ə fekt′) what happens as the result of a cause (p. 149, 277)

electric charge (i lek′trik chärj) tiny amount of energy in the particles of matter (p. 374)

electric circuit (i lek′trik sėr′kit) the path that a controlled electric current flows through (p. 376)

electric current (i lek′trik kėr′ənt) the movement of an electric charge from one place to another (p. 376)

element (el′ə mənt) matter that has only one kind of atom (p. 282)

energy (en′ ər jē) the ability to do work or to cause a change (p. 359)

environment (en vī′rən mənt) everything that surrounds a living thing (p. 71)

equator (i kwā′ tər) the imaginary line that separates the north and south halves of Earth (p. 429)

erosion (i rō′ zhən) the movement of weathered materials (p. 232)

estimating and measuring (es′tə māt ing and mezh′ər ing) to tell what you think an object's measurements are and then to measure it in units (p. 210)

evaporation (i vap′ ə rā′ shən) the changing of a liquid into a gas (p. 157)

experiment (ek sper′ə ment) to formulate and test a hypothesis using a scientific method (p. 140)

explore (ek splôr′) to study a scientific idea in a hands-on manner (p. 36)

extinct (ek stingkt′) no longer lives on Earth (p. 23)

food chain (füd chān) the movement of energy from one type of living thing to another (p. 108)

food web (füd web) the flow of energy between food chains which ties a community together (p. 108)

force (fôrs) a push or a pull (p. 332)

forming questions and hypotheses (fôrm′ing kwes′chənz and hī poth′ə sēz′) to think of how you can solve a problem or answer a question (p. 140)

fossil (fos′ əl) remains or mark of a living thing from long ago (p. 22)

friction (frik′ shən) a contact force that opposes the motion of an object (p. 333)

gas (gas) the form of matter which has no shape, has particles that are not connected to each other, and takes up whatever space is available (p. 281)

germinate (jėr′ mə nāt) begins to grow (p. 20)

germs (jėrmz) small living things that include bacteria and viruses, many of which can cause illness (p. 126)

grassland (gras′ land′) land ecosystem that has many grasses and few trees (p. 76)

gravity (grav′ə tē) a non-contact force that pulls objects toward each other (p. 336)

groundwater (ground′ wȯ′ tər) water that has slowly made its way through soil and then collects in spaces between underground rock; it is brought to the surface by digging wells (p. 155)

habitat (hab′ə tat) the place where a living thing makes its home (p. 72)

heat (hēt) the transfer of thermal energy from one piece of matter to another (p. 366)

herbivore (ėr′bə vôr) living things that eat only plants (p. 106)

hibernate (hī′bər nāt) to spend winter resting; body systems slow down in order to save energy (p. 52)

hurricane (hėr′ə kān) a huge, strong storm that forms over the ocean (p. 182)

identifying and controlling variables (ī den′tə fī ing and kən trōl′ ing vâr′ē ə bəlz) to change one thing, but keep all the other factors the same (p. 40)

igneous rock (ig′nē əs rok′) rock that forms when melted earth materials cool and harden (p. 200)

inclined plane (in klīnd′ plān) a slanting surface that connects a lower level to a higher level (p. 340)

inference (in′fər əns) a conclusion based on facts, experiences, observations, or knowledge (p. 173)

inferring (in fėr′ ing) to draw a conclusion or make a reasonable guess based on what you have learned or what you know (p. 100)

inherited (in her′it əd) passed on from parent to offspring (p. 48)

interpreting data (in tėr′prit ing dā′tə) to use the information you have collected to solve problems or answer questions (p. 26)

invention (in ven′ shən) something that has been made for the first time (p. 479)

investigate (in ves′ tə gāt) to solve a problem or answer a question by following an existing procedure or an original one (p. 26)

investigating and experimenting (in ves′ tə gāt ing and ek sper′ə ment ing) to plan and do an investigation to test a hypothesis or solve a problem (p. 508)

kinetic energy (ki net′ik en′ər jē) energy of motion (p. 361)

landform (land′ fôrm) a natural feature on the surface of Earth's crust (p. 224)

larva (lär′ və) stage in an insect's life after it hatches from the egg (p. 45)

lava (lä′ və) hot, molten rock on Earth's surface (p. 226)

lever (lev′ər) a simple machine used to lift and move things (p. 341)

life cycle (līf sī′kəl) the stages through which an organism passes between birth and death (p. 44)

light (līt) a form of energy that can be seen (p. 370)

liquid (lik′wid) matter that does not have a definite shape but takes up a definite amount of space (p. 280)

loam (lōm) soil that contains a mixture of humus and mineral materials of sand, silt, and clay (p. 209)

lunar eclipse (lü′nər i klips′) Earth's shadow moving across the Moon (p. 434)

magma (mag′mə) hot, molten rock that forms deep underground (p. 226)

magnetic (mag net′ik) having the property to pull on, or attract, metals that have iron in them (p. 337)

magnetism (mag′nə tiz′əm) a non-contact force that pulls objects containing iron (p. 337)

main idea (mān ī dē′ə) what a paragraph is about; the most important idea (p. 69, 357)

making operational definitions (māk′ ing op′ə rā′ shən əl def′ə nish′ənz) to define or describe an object or event based on your own experience (p. 68)

making and using models (māk′ ing and yüz′ ing mod′lz) to make a model from materials or to make a sketch or a diagram (p. 36)

mantle (man′tl) the middle layer of Earth (p. 223)

mass (mas) amount of matter (p. 284)

matter (mat′ər) anything that takes up space and has mass (p. 279)

metamorphic rock (met′ ə môr′ fik rok′) rock that forms when existing rock is changed by heat and pressure (p. 200)

migrate (mī′ grāt) to move to another place to find better climate, food, or a mate (p. 52)

mineral (min′ ər əl) natural material that forms from nonliving matter (p. 199)

mixture (miks′ chər) two or more kinds of matter that are placed together but can be easily separated (p. 306)

Moon (mün) the natural satellite that orbits around Earth (p. 432)

Moon phase (mün fāz) the way the Moon looks because of the amount of the lit side of the Moon that can be seen from Earth at the same time (p. 434)

motion (mō′shən) a change in the position of an object (p. 327)

natural resources (nach′ ər əl ri sôrs′əz) natural materials, such as soil, wood, water, air, oil, or minerals, that living things need (p. 247)

nonrenewable resources (non ri nü′ə bəl ri sôrs′ əz) resource that cannot be replaced once it is used up (p. 248)

nutrient (nü′ trē ənt) thing plants need in order to grow (p. 206)

observing (əb zėrv′ ing) using your senses to find out about objects, events, or living things (p. 4)

omnivore (om′ nə vôr′) living things that eat plants and other animals for food (p. 106)

orbit (ôr′ bit) the path of any object in space that revolves around another object in space (p. 456)

periodic table (pir′ē od′ik tā′bəl) an arrangement of elements based on their properties (p. 283)

physical change (fiz′ ə kəl chānj) a change that makes matter look different without becoming a new substance (p. 303)

pitch (pich) how high or low a sound is (p. 392)

planet (plan′it) a large body of matter that revolves, or travels, around any star (p. 456)

pollinate (pol′ ə nāt) move pollen from the part of a flower that makes pollen to the part of a flower that makes seeds (p. 15)

pollution (pə lü′ shən) waste materials that make the environment dirty (p. 124)

population (pop′ yə lā′ shən) all the living things of the same kind that live in the same place at the same time (p. 74)

position (pə zish′ ən) the location of an object (p. 327)

potential energy (pə ten′shəl en′ ər jē) the energy something has because of its position (p. 360)

precipitation (pri sip′ə tā′ shən) water that falls to Earth as rain, hail, sleet, or snow (p. 159)

predator (pred′ə tər) a consumer that hunts other animals for food (p. 107)

predicting (pri dikt′ ing) to tell what you think will happen (p. 162)

pressure (presh′ər) force per unit area that is applied to a substance (p. 281)

prey (prā) any animal that is hunted by others for food (p. 107)

producer (prə dü′sər) living things that make their own food (p. 106)

property (prop′ər tē) something about matter that you can observe with one or more of your senses (p. 279)

pulley (pul′ē) a machine that changes the direction of motion of an object to which a force is applied (p. 343)

pupa (pyü′pə) stage in an insect's life between larva and adult (p. 45)

recycle (rē sī′kəl) treat or process something so it can be used again (p. 254)

reflect (ri flekt′) to bounce off of (p. 372)

refract (ri frakt′) to bend (p. 372)

relative position (rel′ə tiv pə zish′ən) a change in an object's position compared to another object (p. 329)

renewable resource (ri nü′ ə bəl ri sôrs′) resource that is endless like sunlight, or that is naturally replaced in a fairly short time, such as trees (p. 247)

resource (ri sôrs′) See Natural Resources, Renewable Resources, Nonrenewable Resources

revolution (rev′ə lü′ shən) one complete trip around the Sun (p. 428)

rock (rok) natural, solid, nonliving material made of one or more minerals (p. 199)

rotation (rō tā′ shən) one complete spin on an axis (p. 425)

scientific method (sī′ən tif′ik meth′əd) organized ways of finding answers and solving problems (p. xxvi)

sedimentary rock (sed′ə men′tər ē rok′) rock that forms when small pieces of earth materials collect and become bound together (p. 200)

seed leaf (sēd lēf) part of a seed that has stored food (p. 20)

seedling (sēd′ ling) a new, small plant that grows from a seed (p. 20)

sequence (sē′kwəns) the order in which events take place (p. 37, 221, 421, 477)

soil (soil) the part of Earth's surface consisting of humus and weathered rock in which plants grow (p. 206)

solid (sol′id) matter that has a definite shape and takes up a definite amount of space (p. 280)

solar system (sō′lər sis′təm) the Sun, the nine planets and their moons, and other objects that revolve around the Sun (p. 456)

solution (sə lü′shən) a mixture in which one or more substances dissolves in another (p. 308)

speed (spēd) the rate at which an object changes position (p. 330)

star (stär) a massive ball of hot gases that produces its own light (p. 423)

states of matter (stāts uv mat′ər) the forms of matter – solid, liquid, and gas (p. 304)

summarize (sum′ə rīz′) to cover the main ideas or details in a sentence or two (p. 325)

Sun (sun) our star; a huge ball of hot, glowing gases (p. 424)

system (sis′təm) a set of parts that interact with one another (p. 8)

technology (tek nol′ə jē) the use of science knowledge to invent tools and new ways of doing things (p. 479)

telescope (tel′ə skōp) a tool that gathers lots of light and magnifies objects that are far away and makes faint stars easier to see (p. 436)

thermal energy (thėr′məl en′ər jē) the total kinetic energy of all the particles that make up matter (p. 366)

tool (tül) an object used to do work (p. 479)

tornado (tôr nā′ dō) a rotating column of air that touches the ground and causes damage with its high winds (p. 182)

trait (trāt) a feature passed on to a living thing from its parents (p. 40)

tundra (tun′drə) land ecosystem that is cold and dry (p. 80)

vertebrate (vėr′tə brit) animal with a backbone (p. 40)

vibration (vī brā′shən) a very quick back-and-forth movement (p. 392)

volcano (vol kā′nō) an opening in the Earth's crust from which hot, melted material erupts (p. 226)

volume (vol′yəm) amount of space matter takes up (p. 285)

water cycle (wȯ′tər sī′kəl) the movement of water from Earth's surface into the air and back again (p. 158)

water vapor (wȯ′tər vā′pər) water in the form of an invisible gas in the air (p. 154)

weather (weŦH′ər) what it is like outside including temperature, wind, clouds, and precipitation (p. 175)

weathering (weŦH′ər ing) any process that changes rocks by breaking them into smaller pieces (p. 230)

wetland (wet′land′) low land ecosystem that is covered by water at least part of the time during the year; marshes and swamps are wetlands (p. 86)

wheel and axle (wēl and ak′səl) a simple machine made of a wheel and a rod joined to the center of the wheel (p. 342)

work (wėrk) what happens when a force moves an object over a distance (p. 338)

Index

This index lists the pages on which topics appear in this book. Page numbers after a *p* refer to a photograph or drawing. Page numbers after a *c* refer to a chart, graph, or diagram.

Germinate, 2, p2, 3, 20, p21, 26–27, 28–29

Glacier, p224, 231, p231

Glass
recycled, p254–255, 254–255

Global Positioning System (GPS), 484

Gneiss, p201

Gold, 203

Golden eagle, 104, 109

GPS. *See* Global Positioning System (GPS)

Gram, 284

Granite, p201, c205

Graphic Organizer, c5, c31, c37, c63, c95, c101, c133, c149, c167, c173, c189, c197, c215, c221, 229, c239, c245, c263, c277, c301, c319, c325, c349, c357, c383, c389, c407, c453, c477, c502

Grass, p11, 76

Grassland, 76–77, p77
climate in, c76
comparing data about, p92, 92–93, p93

Grass seeds, 68

Gravity, p322, 336, p336, 336–337, 361, 460
in space, 350–351, p350–351

Great Barrier Reef, p89

Great Plains food web, 108, p108

Great Red Spot (Jupiter), p462

Green plants, 106

Ground squirrels, 74, c75

Groundwater, p146, 155, p158–159

Groupings of animals, 39–43

Groups
in ecosystems, 74, c75
living in, 104

Grow best, 68

Growth stage, c44

Guided Inquiry, Investigate, 26–27, 58–59, 90–91, 128–129, 162–163, 184–185, 210–211, 234–235, 258–259, 290–291, 314–315, 344–345, 378–379, 402–403, 440–441, 466–467, 498–499

Habitats, 72

Hail, 159

Halite, c205

Hand lens, 289, p289

Hardness of minerals, 203, c203

Hawaiian volcano, p227

Health
avoiding germs and, p126, 126–127, p127
foods and, c130, 130–131
maintaining, 124–127
minerals and, 204, c205

Health in Science, 123, 151, 313

Hearing, 400, p400

Heart, 124, p124

Heat, c377
from burning, p370
from electrical heaters, c377

Heat energy, p366, 366–369, p367, p368, p369
matter and, 368
sources of, 367, p367
thermal energy as, 366

Heating and cooling, 480
from solar energy, 494, p494

Hematite, 248, p249

Hemlocks, 118–119

Herbivore, p98, 106, p107

Hexagon, 164

Hibernate, p34, 52, p52

Highways, p486
technology for, 487
tools for building, 487, p487

Hill, p225, p232

Homes
habitats as, 72
technology in, c480, 480–481, p480–481, p482, 482–483, p483

Hoover Dam, p493

Horizon, p425

Horne, Clifton, 408

Housing, p121, 251
See also Shelter

Howard, Ayanna, 472

How to Read Science, xx, xxi, 5, 37, 101, 149, 173, 197, 221, 245, 277, 301, 325, 357, 389, 421, 453, 477; *See also* Target Reading Skills

Hubble Space Telescope, p446, 446–447, p447, 463

Humidity, 177

Humus, 209

Hunting by animals, p53

Credits

Photographs

Cover: ©Flip Nicklin/Minden Pictures, ©David Nardini/Getty Images.

Front Matter: iii Daniel J. Cox/Natural Exposures, (T) Getty Images; v ©Frans Lanting/Minden Pictures; vi ©DK Images; vii (R) ©Randy M. Ury/Corbis, (L) ©Breck P. Kent/Animals Animals/Earth Scenes; viii ©Jack Dykinga/Getty Images; xi ©Douglas Peebles/Corbis; xii ©Lloyd Cluff/Corbis; xv ©RNT Productions/Corbis; xxii ©Timothy O'Keefe/Index Stock Imagery; xxiii Getty Images; xxiv (Bkgd) ©Steve Bloom/Getty Images, (C) ©Robert Sullivan/AFP/Getty Images; xxix Getty Images; xxv ©Frank Greenaway/DK Images; xxviii (BL) Getty Images, (CL) ©Dave King/DK Images; xxx ©Comstock Inc.

Unit Dividers: Unit A (Bkgd) Getty Images, (CC) Digital Vision; Unit B (Bkgd) ©Kim Heacox/Getty Images, (BC) Getty Images; Unit C (Bkgd) ©Lester Lefkowitz/Getty Images; Unit D (Bkgd) Corbis

Chapter 1: 1 (B) ©Wolfgang Kaehler/Corbis, (T, C) Getty Images; 2 (T) ©John Warden/Index Stock Imagery, (BL) ©DK Images, (BL) Getty Images, (BR) ©Nigel Cattlin/Photo Researchers, Inc.; 3 (BL) ©Nigel Cattlin/Holt Studios, (BC) Neg./Transparency no. K13073. Courtesy Dept. of Library Services/American Museum of Natural History; 5 (CR) ©Stone/Getty Images, (Bkgd) ©John Warden/Index Stock Imagery; 6 ©John Warden/Index Stock Imagery; 7 (BR) ©Jim Steinberg/Photo Researchers, Inc., (TR) ©Photographer's Choice/Getty Images; 8 ©DK Images; 9 (CR, TR, BR) ©DK Images, (TC) Getty Images; 10 (R) Silver Burdett Ginn, (TL) Getty Images; 11 ©DK Images; 12 ©Lou Jacobs Jr./Grant Heilman Photography; 13 (TR) ©George Bernard/NHPA Limited, (TR) ©DK Images, (CR) ©TH Foto-Werbung/Photo Researchers, Inc., (TR) ©Niall Benvie/Corbis, (BR) ©The Garden Picture Library/Alamy Images; 14 (BL) ©Stone/Getty Images, (BR) ©Jeff Lepore/Photo Researchers, Inc., (TL) ©Peter Smithers/Corbis; 15 (BR) ©DK Images, (TL) Getty Images, 16 (B) ©Carolina Biological/Visuals Unlimited, (TL) Getty Images; 17 (CL) ©M & C Photography/Peter Arnold, Inc., (TR) ©Brad Mogen/Visuals Unlimited, (TC) ©Pat O'Hara/Corbis, (CL) ©Wally Eberhart/Visuals Unlimited, (BR) ©DK Images; 18 (BC) ©Darryl Torckler/Getty Images, (CC) ©Brian Gordon Green/NGS Image Collection, (BC) ©John Poutier/Maxx Images, Inc., (BC) ©Jorg & Petra Wegner/Animals Animals/Earth Scenes, (TL) ©DK Images; 19 (L) ©DK Images, (CR) ©Steve Bloom Images/Alamy Images; 21 (CL) ©DK Images, (CR) Nigel Cattlin/Holt Studios, (BC) ©Kenneth W. Fink/Photo Researchers, Inc., (BC) ©Nigel Cattlin/Photo Researchers, Inc.; 23 (TR) ©Dr. E. R. Degginger/Color-Pic, Inc., (CL) ©John Cancalosi/Peter Arnold, Inc., (TL) Neg./Transparency no. K13073. Courtesy Dept. of Library Services/American Museum of Natural History, (BR) ©David Muench/Muench

Photography, Inc, (CR) ©James L. Amos/Corbis; 24 (BL) ©The Natural History Museum, London, (BR, TL) ©DK Images; 26 ©Ed Young/Corbis; 28 (TR) ©Dennis MacDonald/PhotoEdit, (CR) ©Inga Spence/Visuals Unlimited, (CR) ©Steven Emery/Index Stock Imagery, (BR) ©Comstock Inc.; 31 (TL) ©DK Images, (TR) ©Kenneth W. Fink/Photo Researchers, Inc.; 32 (Bkgd) ©MSFC/NASA, (TL, BR) NASA; **Chapter 2:** 33 (B) ©Barbara Von Hoffmann/Animals Animals/Earth Scenes, (Bkgd) ©David Harrison/Index Stock Imagery; 34 (BL) ©David L. Shirk/Animals Animals/Earth Scenes, (T) ©Tom Brakefield/Corbis, (BR) ©Jeff L. Lepore/Photo Researchers, Inc.; 35 (BL, BR) ©Brad Mogen/Visuals Unlimited; 37 (C) ©David Stover/ImageState, (Bkgd) ©Tom Brakefield/Corbis; 38 ©Tom Brakefield/Corbis; 39 (BR) ©Tom Vezo/Nature Picture Library, (BC) ©Zefa/Masterfile Corporation, (BL) ©Taxi/Getty Images, (BC) ©Natural Visions/Alamy Images, (TR) ©Frans Lanting/Minden Pictures; 40 (B) ©Tom Brakefield/Bruce Coleman Inc., (TL) ©Randy M. Ury/Corbis, 41 (CR) ©DK Images, (BC) ©Jim Brandenburg/Minden Pictures, (BR) ©Frans Lanting/Minden Pictures, (CR) Getty Images, (CR) ©Ken Lucas/Visuals Unlimited; 42 ©David Aubrey/Corbis; 43 (TR) ©Danny Lehman/Corbis, (TR) ©Robert Pickett, (CR) ©The Image Bank/Getty Images, (BR) ©Brian Rogers/Visuals Unlimited; 44 (TL, TR) ©DK Images, (BR) ©Charles Melton/Visuals Unlimited; 45 (B) ©Brad Mogen/Visuals Unlimited, (T) ©Dick Scott/Visuals Unlimited; 46 (CL) ©Bettmann/Corbis, (BL) ©Keren Su/China Span/Alamy Images, (TL) ©Zefa/Masterfile Corporation; 47 (TR) ©Carolina Biological Supply Company/Phototake, (CL, BL) ©DK Images, (BL) ©Breck P. Kent/Animals Animals/Earth Scenes, (BR) ©Randy M. Ury/Corbis; 48 (BR) ©DK Images, (TR) ©Ken Lucas/Visuals Unlimited, (TL) ©Tony Evans/Timelapse Library/Getty Images; 49 (CL) ©Frans Lanting/Minden Pictures, (TR) ©Kevin Schafer/Corbis, (CR) ©Gary W. Carter/Corbis, (BR) ©DK Images; 50 ©Vittoriano Rastelli/Corbis, (TL) ©Photodisc Green/Getty Images; 51 (T) ©Rod Planck/Photo Researchers, Inc., (CC) ©James Robinson/Animals Animals/Earth Scenes, (TR) ©Michael Quinton/Minden Pictures, (TR) ©Chris Newbert/Minden Pictures, (CL) ©The Image Bank/Getty Images, (BL) ©Rolf Kopfle/Bruce Coleman Inc., (BC) ©Tim Laman/NGS Image Collection, (BC) ©Suzanne L. & Joseph T. Collins/Photo Researchers, Inc., (CC) ©Steve E. Ross/Photo Researchers, Inc., (TC) ©Ken Wilson/Papilio/Corbis, (CR) ©David Aubrey/Corbis, (BR) ©E. R. Degginger/Bruce Coleman, Inc., (BL) ©Rick & Nora Bowers/Visuals Unlimited; 52 (TR) ©DK Images, (BR) ©George Grall/NGS Image Collection, (BR) ©Jeff L. Lepore/Photo Researchers, Inc., (TL) ©Eric and David Hosking/Corbis, (TL) ©Photodisc Blue/Getty Images; 53 (T) ©Gerry Ellis/Minden Pictures, (B) ©Terry W. Eggers/Corbis; 54 (TL) ©James L. Amos/Photo Researchers, Inc., (B) ©DK Images, (CL) ©Layne Kennedy/Corbis; 55 (TL) ©DK Images, (TR) ©Breck P. Kent/Animals Animals/Earth Scenes; 56 (R) ©Breck P. Kent/Animals Animals/Earth Scenes, (B) Senekenberg Nature Museum/©DK Images, (TL) Colin Keates/Courtesy of the Natural History Museum, London/©DK Images; 57 ©Ross M. Horowitz/Getty Images; 58 ©Larry L. Miller/Photo Researchers, Inc.; 60 Digital Vision; 61 ©Masa Ushioda/Visual & Written/Bruce Coleman, Inc.; 63 ©DK Images; 64 (T) ©Dutheil Didier/SYGMA/Corbis, (BL) ©Reuters/Corbis; **Chapter 3:** 65 (Bkgd) Getty Images, (T) ©Photodisc Green/Getty Images; 66 (T) ©Mark E. Gibson Stock Photography, (BL) ©J. Eastcott/Y. Eastcott Film/NGS Image Collection, (BR) ©Enzo & Paolo Ragazzini/Corbis; 67 (BL) ©Andy Binns/Ecoscene, (BR)

©Jim Zipp/Photo Researchers, Inc., (CR) ©Alan Carey/Photo Researchers, Inc., (TR) ©Steve Kaufman/Corbis; 69 ©Mark E. Gibson Stock Photography; 70 ©Mark E. Gibson Stock Photography; 71 ©Siede Preis/Getty Images; 72 Getty Images; 73 (Bkgd) ©Melissa Farlow/Aurora & Quanta Productions, (TC) ©DK Images, (BC) ©Kurt Stier/Corbis; 74 (CL) ©Royalty-Free/Corbis, (BL) ©Alan Carey/Photo Researchers, Inc.; 75 (CR) ©Joseph Van Os/Getty Images, (L) ©Kennan Ward/Corbis, (BR) Darren Bennett/Animals Animals/Earth Scenes; 76 ©OSF/Animals Animals/Earth Scenes; 77 (T) ©Enzo & Paolo Ragazzini/Corbis, (BL) ©Jason Edwards/NGS Image Collection, (BR) ©Steve Kaufman/Corbis; 78 (BL) ©Jack Dykinga/Getty Images, (BR) Jerry Young/©DK Images, (TL) ©DK Images; 79 (Bkgd) ©J. Eastcott/Y. Eastcott Film/NGS Image Collection, (TL) Daniel J. Cox/Natural Exposures; 80 (BL) Daniel J. Cox/Natural Exposures, (BR) ©Ed Reschke/Peter Arnold, Inc.; 81 (L) ©Andy Binns/Ecoscene, (TR, CL, CR) Daniel J. Cox/Natural Exposures; 82 ©Tim Laman/NGS Image Collection; 83 (TR) ©Michio Hoshino/Minden Pictures, (TL, BR) ©Jim Brandenburg/Minden Pictures, (BL) ©Jay Dickman/Corbis, (CR) ©David Ulmer/Stock Boston; 84 (CR) ©Roy Toft/NGS Image Collection, (TR) ©Claus Meyer/Minden Pictures, (BR) ©Ken Preston-Mafham/Animals Animals/Earth Scenes, (TL) Alamy; 85 (BL) ©Michael & Patricia Fogden/Minden Pictures, (T) ©Tui De Roy/Minden Pictures; 86 (B) Daniel J. Cox/Natural Exposures, (TR) ©Jim Zipp/Photo Researchers, Inc., (TL) ©Roy Toft/NGS Image Collection; 87 (Bkgd) Daniel J. Cox/Natural Exposures, (TR) ©Joseph H. Bailey/NGS Image Collection; 88 (TL) ©Medford Taylor/NGS Image Collection, (BR) ©Fred Bavendam/Peter Arnold, Inc.; 89 (TR) ©Mick Turner/PhotoLibrary, (Bkgd) ©Royalty-Free/Corbis; 90 Getty Images; 95 ©Ken Preston-Mafham/Animals Animals/Earth Scenes; 96 ©Bettmann/Corbis; **Chapter 4:** 97 ©M. Colbeck/OSF/Animals Animals/Earth Scenes; 98 (T) ©Stephen Frink/Corbis, (BL) ©Carol Havens/Corbis, (BR) ©K. H. Haenel/Zefa/Masterfile Corporation; 99 (BL) ©D. Robert and Lorri Franz/Corbis, (TR) ©Jim Brandenburg/Minden Pictures, (CR) ©Dr. Gopal Murti/Photo Researchers, Inc., (BR) ©Gerald Hinde/ABPL/Animals Animals/Earth Scenes; 101 (CR) ©Richard Walters/Visuals Unlimited, (Bkgd) ©Stephen Frink/Corbis, (BR) ©Bob Marsh/Papilio/Corbis, (CC) ©David Boag/Alamy Images; 102 ©Stephen Frink/Corbis; 103 (CR) Brand X Pictures, (BR) ©Patti Murray/Earth Scenes/Maxx Images, Inc., (CR) ©Laura Sivell/Papilio/Corbis, (BR) Getty Images; 104 (B) ©Richard Kolar/Animals Animals/Earth Scenes, (T) ©Rick Raymond/Index Stock Imagery; 105 (T) ©Michael & Patricia Fogden/Corbis, (B) ©B. Jones/M. Shimlock/Photo Researchers, Inc.; 106 (BL) ©Chase Swift/Corbis, (BC) ©Carol Havens/Corbis, (BR) ©Frank Blackburn/Ecoscene/Corbis, (TL) ©Hope Ryden/NGS Image Collection; 107 (B) ©D. Robert and Lorri Franz/Corbis, (TL) ©K. H. Haenel/Zefa/Masterfile Corporation, (CL) ©Randy Wells/Corbis, (BL) ©Danny Lehman/Corbis; 108 (TL, BL) Getty Images, (BR) ©Yva Momatiuk/John Eastcott/Minden Pictures, (BC) ©Naturfoto Honal/Corbis, (CC) ©Kevin R. Morris/Corbis; 109 (C) Minden Pictures, (R) ©Claudia Adams/Alamy Images, (BL) ©Tom Brakefield/Corbis; 110 (T) ©Gerry Ellis/Minden Pictures, (BL) ©Michael & Patricia Fogden/Corbis, (BL) ©Martin Harvey/Photo Researchers, Inc., (TL) ©Photodisc Green/Getty Images; 111 ©Gerald Hinde/ABPL/Animals Animals/Earth Scenes; 112 (T) ©DK Images, (CL) ©Raymond Gehman/Corbis, (BL) ©Scott Camazine/Photo Researchers, Inc.; 113 ©Paal Hermansen/

NHPA Limited; 114 (BR) ©Richard H. Johnston/Getty Images, (BL) ©Harry Engels/Photo Researchers, Inc.; 115 (TR) ©The Image Bank/Getty Images, (CR) ©Bob Daemmrich/SYGMA/Corbis, (B) ©Ed Bock/Corbis; 116 (B) ©Gary Braasch/Corbis, (TL) ©Lawrence Lawry/Getty Images; 117 (TR) ©Christian Grzimek/Okapia/Photo Researchers, Inc., (CR) ©Raymond Gehman/NGS Image Collection, (BR) ©Phil Schermeister/NGS Image Collection, (BL) ©Philip James Corwin/Corbis, (BC) ©Carol Cohen/Corbis; 118 (T) ©Bruce Forster/Getty Images, (B) ©Bruce Hands/Stock Boston; 119 (T) ©Jim Brandenburg/Minden Pictures, (B) ©Charles Mauzy/Corbis; 120 (L) ©G. Biss/Masterfile Corporation, (TL) ©Brand X Pictures/Getty Images; 121 (TL) Corbis, (CL) ©Steve Cole/Masterfile Corporation, (C) ©Sandy Felsenthal/Corbis, (BR) ©Terry W. Eggers/Corbis; 122 Getty Images; 124 (B) Getty Images, (TL) Rubberball Productions; 126 (BR) ©DK Images, (TR) ©Dr. Gopal Murti/Photo Researchers, Inc.; 127 (BL) ©S. Lowry/Univ. Ulster/Getty Images, (TL) ©Institut Pasteur/Phototake; 128 Corbis; 133 Minden Pictures; 134 (TL) NASA, (L) ©Time Life Pictures/NASA/Getty Images; 135 (B) NASA, (T) Stephen Oliver/©DK Images; 136 (TL) ©Jim Sugar/Corbis, (Bkgd) Getty Images, (BL) Creatas; 140 ©Gary W. Carter/Corbis; 144 (C) Frank Greenaway/©DK Images, (Bkgd) ©Rex Butcher/Bruce Coleman Inc. **Chapter 5:** 145 ©Pablo Corral Vega/Corbis; 146 ©Jim Brandenburg/Minden Pictures; 147 (BR) ©Carson Baldwin Jr./Animals Animals/Earth Scenes, (BR) Aflo Foto Agency; 149 (CL) ©Susan Leavines/Photo Researchers, Inc., (Bkgd) ©Jim Brandenburg/Minden Pictures; 150 ©Jim Brandenburg/Minden Pictures; 151 (T) ©Manfred Kage/Peter Arnold, Inc., (TL) ©Goddard Space Flight Center/NOAA/NASA Image Exchange; 152 (TL) ©Photodisc Green/Getty Images, (B) Grant Heilman Photography; 153 (TL) ©Richard Herrmann/Visuals Unlimited, (TR) ©Beverly Joubert/NGS Image Collection, (CR) ©David R. Frazier/Photo Researchers, Inc., (BL) ©Geoff Tompkinson/Photo Researchers, Inc., (BR) ©Richard Cummins/Lonely Planet Images; 154 (TL, BR) ©Goddard Space Flight Center/NOAA/NASA Image Exchange; 155 (CR) ©Wolfgang Kaehler/Corbis, (BR) ©EyeWire, Inc./Getty Images, (TR) ©M. Timothy O'Keefe/Bruce Coleman, Inc.; 156 (BL) ©Richard Megna/Fundamental Photographs, (BR) ©Michael P. Gadomski/Photo Researchers, Inc., (TL, BC) ©Dave King/DK Images; 157 (TR) ©Michael P. Godomski/Photo Researchers, Inc., (BR) Aflo Foto Agency, (CR) ©Dave King/DK Images; 158 ©Carson Baldwin Jr./Animals Animals/Earth Scenes; 159 ©The Image Bank/Getty Images; 160 (BL) ©James Keyser/Time Life Pictures/Getty Images, (BR) Photri-Microstock, (TL) ©Michael Keller/Corbis; 161 ©Dennis Light/Light Photographic; 162 ©P. Jude/Photo Researchers, Inc.; 164 (B) ©Richard Walters/Visuals Unlimited, (Bkgd) ©Garry Black/Masterfile Corporation; 165 (T) ©M. Kulyk/Photo Researchers, Inc., (C) ©Stone/Getty Images, (B) ©Claude Nuridsany & Marie Perennou/Photo Researchers, Inc.; 167 ©Richard Megna/Fundamental Photographs; 168 (BL) ©Volker Steger/Photo Researchers, Inc., (T) ©Manuel Lazcano/Jean-Michel Cousteau Productions/AP/Wide World Photos, (Bkgd) ©Photodisc Green/Getty Images; **Chapter 6:** 169 ©Macduff Everton/Corbis; 170 (T) ©John Lund/Corbis, (B) ©The Image Bank/Getty Images, (BR) ©Allan Davey/Masterfile Corporation; 171 ©Boden/Ledingham/Masterfile Corporation; 173 (CR) ©D. Boone/Corbis, (Bkgd) ©John Lund/Corbis; 174 ©John Lund/Corbis; 175 (TR) ©Leonard Lessin/Peter Arnold, Inc., (TL) ©Royalty-Free/Corbis; 177 (CR) ©DK Images, (BR) ©Carol

Havens/Corbis, (TR) ©Leonard Lessin/Peter Arnold, Inc.; 178 ©Guy Motil/Corbis; 179 (BR) ©Tom Uhlman/Visuals Unlimited, (TL) ©NOAA/Getty Images, (TR) Corbis; 180 (CL) ©Julie Eggers/Bruce Coleman, Inc., (T) ©Steve Solum/Bruce Coleman, Inc., (TL) ©Todd A. Gipstein/Corbis; 181 (TR, CR) Tom Bean; 182 (TC) ©The Image Bank/Getty Images, (R) ©Allan Davey/Masterfile Corporation, (TL) ©Jim Zuckerman/Corbis; 183 (TR) ©Terry Renna/AP/Wide World Photos, (CR) ©Tom Uhlman/Visuals Unlimited, (BR) Digital Vision, (CR) ©Boden/Ledingham/Masterfile Corporation; 184 ©Jim Zuckerman/Corbis; 186 (Bkgd) ©Neil Rabinowitz/Corbis, (TR) ©Andre Jenny/Alamy Images, (CR) ©Indianapolis Star-Frank Espich/AP/Wide World Photos, (CL) ©G. Renner/Robert Harding Picture Library Ltd., (B) ©Ted S. warren/AP/Wide World Photos; 189 (TR) ©DK Images, (TR) ©Leonard Lessin/Peter Arnold, Inc.; 190 (Bkgd) ©The Image Bank/Getty Images, (BR) ©image100/Alamy, (CL) ©Royalty-Free/Corbis, (BL) ©Joyce Photographics/Photo Researchers, Inc.; 191 (CL, CR) ©Wolfgang Kaehler/Corbis; 192 (TL) ©Noel Hendrickson/Masterfile Corporation, (Bkgd) ©Royalty-Free/Corbis, (CL) ©Ron Stroud/Masterfile Corporation; **Chapter 7:** 193 ©Mark Newman/Lonely Planet Images; 194 (T) ©J. A. Kraulis/Masterfile Corporation, (BL, BC) ©DK Images, (BR) ©Andrew J. Martinez/Photo Researchers, Inc.; 195 ©DK Images; 197 (Bkgd) ©J. A. Kraulis/Masterfile Corporation, (Insets) ©DK Images, (Inset) ©Andrew J. Martinez/Photo Researchers, Inc.; 198 ©J. A. Kraulis/Masterfile Corporation; 199 DK Images; 200 (Inset) Royal Museum of Scotland/©DK Images, (Inset) Getty Images, (Inset, TL) ©DK Images, (B) ©Douglas Peebles/Corbis; 201 (TL, TR, BR) ©DK Images, (BL) ©Andrew J. Martinez/Photo Researchers, Inc.; 202 (CR) ©Breck P. Kent/Animals Animals/Earth Scenes, (TL) ©DK Images, (B) ©Carey B. Van Loon; 203 (CL, BL) ©DK Images; 204 ©Tim Pannell/Corbis; 205 (TL) ©M. Claye/Jacana Scientific Control/Photo Researchers, Inc., (TCL) ©Ross Frid/Visuals Unlimited, (CL, BL) ©DK Images, (CR) Getty Images, (CR) ©Royalty-Free/Corbis; 206 (T) ©Jeremy Burgess/Science Photo Library/Photo Researchers, Inc., (C) ©G. I. Bernard/Animals Animals/Earth Scenes, (B) ©Dr. Parvinder Sethi, (TL) ©The Image Bank/Getty Images; 207 ©Peter Hulme/Ecoscene/Corbis; 208 (BL) ©Royalty-Free/Corbis, (TL) ©Comstock, Inc.; 210 ©ThinkStock/SuperStock; 212 (Bkgd) Brand X Pictures, (BL) ©Michael Fogden/Animals Animals/Earth Scenes, (BR) ©Jeremy Burgess/Science Photo Library/Photo Researchers, Inc.; 213 (CR) Getty Images, (BL) ©Jacob Halaska/Index Stock Imagery; 215 ©DK Images; 216 (TL, BL) ©Goddard Space Center/NASA; **Chapter 8:** 217 ©David Muench/Corbis; 218 ©Robert Madden/NGS Image Collection; 219 (BL) ©Jeremy Horner/Corbis, (BR) ©William Manning/Corbis; 221 (CR) Corbis, (Bkgd) ©Robert Madden/NGS Image Collection; 222 ©Robert Madden/NGS Image Collection; 223 ©Jim Sugar/Corbis; 224 (TL) ©Daryl Benson/Masterfile Corporation, (BR) ©Bruce Burkhardt/Corbis; 225 (TR) ©David Muench/Corbis, (BL) ©Pat O'Hara/Corbis, (TC) ©Royalty-Free/Corbis; 226 ©Photographer's Choice/Getty Images, (TL) ©Jim Sugar/Corbis; 227 ©Jim Sugar/Corbis; 228 (TL, B) ©Lloyd Cluff/Corbis; 229 (TR) ©Ken M. John/Photo Researchers, Inc., (CR) ©Spencer Grant/Photo Researchers, Inc., (BR) ©La Prensa Grafica/AP/Wide World Photos; 230 (L) ©Fred Whitehead/Animals Animals/Earth Scenes, (TL) Brand X Pictures; 231 (R) Natural History Museum/©DK Images, (B) ©Jeremy Horner/Corbis; 232 (C) ©Kelly-Mooney Photography/Corbis, (TL) ©Mario Fantin/Photo Researchers, Inc., (T)

©DK Images, (B) ©Stone/Getty Images; 233 ©William Manning/Corbis; 234 ©Cindy Kassab/Corbis; 236 (Bkgd) ©Ethel Davis/ImageState, (TR) ©Bettmann/Corbis, (CR) ©Ken M. John/Photo Researchers, Inc., (BR) ©Popperfoto/Alamy Images; 239 (TR) Natural History Museum/©DK Images, (TR) ©Jeremy Horner/Corbis; 240 (CL) NASA, (B) Getty Images; **Chapter 9:** 241 ©Peter Walton/Index Stock Imagery; 242 (BR) ©Jim Wark/Index Stock Imagery, (T) ©Galen Rowell/Corbis, (BL) ©Taxi/Getty Images; 243 (BL) ©Alan Towse/Ecoscene/Corbis, (BR) ©Hal Lott/Corbis; 245 (CL) ©David M. Dennis/Animals Animals/Earth Scenes, (Bkgd) ©Galen Rowell/Corbis; 246 ©Galen Rowell/Corbis; 247 (T) ©Taxi/Getty Images, (B) Digital Vision, (TR) ©Photodisc Green/Getty Images; 248 (BR) ©Mark E. Gibson Stock Photography, (TL) ©Comstock, Inc.; 249 (TR) ©DK Images, (B) Digital Vision, (CR) Richard M. Busch; 250 (BL) ©Kevin Fleming/Corbis, (CR) ©Alan Towse/Ecoscene/Corbis, (TL) ©Jaye Phillips/Index Stock Imagery; 251 (CR) ©Jaye Phillips/Index Stock Imagery, (B) ©Stone/Getty Images; 252 (TR) ©Stone/Getty Images, (TL) Getty Images; 254 (TR) ©James L. Amos/Corbis, (BL) ©Hal Lott/Corbis, (BR) ©Photodisc Blue/Getty Images, (TL) ©Bill Frymire/Masterfile Corporation; 255 (TR) ©DK Images, (BL) ©Jose Azel/Aurora & Quanta Productions, (BC) ©Stephen Barnett/ImageState; 256 (T) ©Eunice Harris/Index Stock Imagery, (B) ©Nick Hawkes; Ecoscene/Corbis, (C) ©Liz Hymans/Corbis, (TL) ©Enzo & Paolo Ragazzini/Corbis; 257 ©Dennis Brack/Black Star; 258 ©Philip James/Corbis; 260 ©Aneal Vohra/Index Stock Imagery; 264 (TL) ©Craig Hammell/Corbis, (CL) ©R. Ian Lloyd/Masterfile Corporation, (B) ©Taxi/Getty Images; 268 ©Paul Nevin/PhotoLibrary; 272 ©Tom McCarthy/PhotoEdit; **Chapter 10:** 273 (Bkgd) ©Taxi/Getty Images; 274 (T) ©Tony Freeman/PhotoEdit, (BR) Getty Images; 277 (CR) ©Photodisc Green/Getty Images, (Bkgd) ©Tony Freeman/PhotoEdit; 278 ©Tony Freeman/PhotoEdit; 279 ©Brand X Pictures/Getty Images; 280 (BL) ©DK Images, (TL) Stephen Oliver/©DK Images; 282 (B) ©Anna Zuckerman-Vdovenko/PhotoEdit, (BR) Getty Images, (TL) Stephen Oliver/©DK Images; 283 Mary Evans Picture Library; 284 ©Comstock/Alamy; 286 Getty Images; 287 (TR) Corbis, (CR) Alamy, (CR) ©Image Source/Alamy; 288 Getty Images; 289 ©Peter Parks/Image Quest Marine; 290 ©Jim Cummins/Corbis; 295 Corbis; 296 (Bkgd) Getty Images; **Chapter 11:** 297 ©The Image Bank/Getty Images; 298 ©Crazy Horse Memorial Foundation; 299 ©DK Images; 301 (Bkgd) ©Crazy Horse Memorial Foundation; 302 ©Crazy Horse Memorial Foundation; 303 Alamy Images; 305 ©Garry Black/Masterfile Corporation; 306 ©Steven Allen/Alamy Images; 308 ©Stone/Getty Images; 310 ©DK Images; 311 (TR) ©Richard Megna/Fundamental Photographs, (CR) Dave King/Pitt Rivers Museum/University of Oxford, Oxford/©DK Images, (B) ©DK Images; 312 (BL) ©Stone/Getty Images, (TL) ©Brand X Pictures/Getty Images; 313 (TR) PhotoLibrary, (B) ©Doug Scott/Age Fotostock; 314 ©Kevin Fleming/Corbis; 320 (TL) ©Shout/Alamy Images, (BL) ©ThinkStock/SuperStock, (Bkgd) ©Stone/Getty Images; **Chapter 12:** 321 ©Allsport Photography/Getty Images; 322 (T) ©Mark A. Johnson/Corbis, (BL) ©Roy Ooms/Masterfile Corporation, (BR) ©Hennie Wiggers/Zefa/Masterfile Corporation; 323 (TR) ©Jim Cummins/Corbis, (BR) ©Taxi/Getty Images; 325 (CL) ©Rubberball Productions/Getty Images, (Bkgd) ©Mark A. Johnson/Corbis; 326 ©Mark A. Johnson/Corbis; 327 (CR) ©David Young-Wolff/PhotoEdit, (TR) ©Royalty-Free/Corbis; 328 ©EuroStyle Graphics/Alamy